LIFE SKILLS

100 THINGS EVERY KID NEEDS TO KNOW

BEFORE LEAVING HOME

By FRANCES VIDAKOVIC

AUTHOR'S NOTE:

FOREWARD

ON CHILDREN

From "The Prophet" By Kahlil Gibran

Your children are not your children.
They are the sons and daughters of Life's longing for itself.
They come through you but not from you,
And though they are with you yet they belong not to you.

You may give them your love but not your thoughts,
For they have their own thoughts.
You may house their bodies but not their souls,
For their souls dwell in the house of tomorrow,
which you cannot visit, not even in your dreams.
You may strive to be like them,
but seek not to make them like you.
For life goes not backward nor tarries with yesterday.

You are the bows from which your children
as living arrows are sent forth.
The archer sees the mark upon the path of the infinite,
and He bends you with His might
that His arrows may go swift and far.
Let your bending in the archer's hand be for gladness;
For even as He loves the arrow that flies,
so He loves also the bow that is stable.

INTRODUCTION

For Parents

Denis Waitley was indeed correct when he said: "The greatest gifts you can give your children are the roots of responsibility and the wings of independence." In this book you will find 100 life skills that every kid would benefit from knowing by the time they're ready to leave home.

Life skills are defined as skills that are necessary or desirable for full participation in everyday day. Technically any skill that is useful can be considered a life skill but they are usually associated with helping us live a better quality of life, so we can accomplish our dreams and live to our full potential.

Because that's our goal of parenting, right? We all want to raise compassionate, independent kids who have the courage, confidence, tenacity and desire to reach their potential. But how do we raise children to be this way: resilient and confident?

Self-confidence rises out of a sense of competence – from a feeling that you can do things, big and small. As a parent, we can encourage a can-do attitude in our children by providing them with as many opportunities to master new skills.

Bottom line is this: you are raising a future adult. You need to equip your kids with the skills they need to survive and prosper in this world. This is one of the greatest gifts you can pass on as a parent.

But please don't wait until your child is on the brink of adulthood to teach them these skills. You need to start as early as you can. Because you know what is even harder than letting your children go? It's not preparing them for the real world.

If your child hasn't learned something, maybe it's because they haven't been taught. It is up to you as a parent to acknowledge if you have been hindering their process of growth by not allowing them to make their own mistakes and discoveries in this world.

The truth is much as you love your children, you will eventually need to let them go. I know, I know, we all wish we could forever protect our kids from the dangers of the world. Only problem is over-parenting sometimes has the opposite effect. Despite our best and most noble intentions, when we over-parent we deprive our kids of the opportunities to learn things on their own. This in turn creates young adults who feel insecure, incapable and unconfident.

So you need to make sure your children have the right tools for this journey. Here in this book you will find 100 useful life skills that your child would benefit greatly from mastering. Feel free to show them the ropes and watch them practice but after that, it is up to them to handle it on their own. Because whether you like it or not, your child will eventually leave home and you need to do what you can to guarantee their greatest chance of success in life.

For the Future Adults of This World

So you are holding a book that purports to contain all the things you need to know before you leave home. Pretty crazy stuff, right? If you're lucky, you may find you have already mastered a few things from this list. If so, that's great! Some are quite simple skills and easy to grasp. Other life skills are more difficult but still worth learning because everything here will help you live a more productive, fulfilling life.

Think now about the things that make you feel confident. When you're truly confident, it means you have faith in your own talents and abilities but not in an arrogant, stuck-up way. Real confidence is instead the belief and quiet inner knowledge that you're capable, despite what other people say.

So how can you begin to feel more capable? Well this road to confidence is paved by daily accomplishments. You don't need to be the smartest kid in the class or most popular to stake your claim on confidence. Focus instead on learning new things and practicing them often until you feel competent enough because competence breeds confidence.

There's no reason why you can't start today. Go out and learn new things! Chase your dreams! They say knowledge is power but once you have it, you need to practice it too. In the words of Dr. Seuss: "You have brains in your head. You have feet in your shoes. You can steer yourself in any direction you choose." So go out there and master these skills today because they will without a doubt help you feel more confident and competent in your life.

LIFE SKILLS LIST

Inside The Home

1. How To Do The Laundry
2. How To Mow The Lawn
3. How To Iron
4. How To Change The Sheets
5. How To Wash The Dishes
6. How To Sew And Mend
7. How To Unclog A Toilet
8. How To Set A Table
9. How To Keep The House Clean
10. How To Do Basic Home Improvements
11. How To Pick Up After Yourself

Outside The Home

12. How To Keep Plants Alive
13. How To Parallel Park
14. How To Build A Campfire
15. How To Order At A Restaurant
16. How To Take Public Transportation
17. How To Be A Respectful House Guest
18. How To Get From A To B
19. How To Take Care Of A Car

Staying Alive

You Need Money To Survive

Time To Be A Grown-Up

Stuff You Just Need To Know

Nothing Wrong With Being A

Smarty Pants

Be An All-Round Gracious, Kind Human Being

81. How To Defuse Potential Conflict
82. How To Advocate For Yourself
83. How To Write A Thank You Letter
84. How To Talk To Strangers
85. How To Have A Conversation With Someone Of Any Age
86. How To Take Responsibility
87. How To Use Your Voice
88. Have Good Social Skills
89. Have Manners
90. Have And Take The Initiative (To Do Stuff!)
91. Understand The Value Of A Mistake
92. How to Let Go of Past Grievances
93. How to Stay Calm
94. How to Not Be Judgmental

Bonus Skills

95. How To Grow Food
96. How To Have Basic Survival Skills
97. How To Speak In Front Of Others
98. Know Your Rights
99. How To Pick The Right Partner

Inside The Home

1. HOW TO DO LAUNDRY

Laundry is a skill every adult needs to know. The great thing is you can be taught how to do this from a young age.

Here are the steps you will need to learn:

- Always check the labels on your clothing first – this is how you will know if your clothes need to be washed in a special way.

- Sort out the dirty clothes into different piles – you will need to separate clothing by colour to prevent discoloration. Make sure you first empty all the pockets so pens, money or paper don't accidentally make their way into the wash. Piles which can be formed include:

  - White or light colours (you may need to soak whites first to make them super white again)

  - Dark colours – which include black, navy, dark green or any shade of red.

  - Towels and washcloths

  - Delicates or underwear

- Treat any heavy stains with a stain remover before washing

- Add detergent – your detergent box or bottle should tell you the right amount of powder to use for your wash load. Add the detergent right at the start – after you put the clothes in the machine, but before you turn the machine on.

- Choose the right cycle for that particular wash – this will vary according to the machine. Understand that different machines have different yet ultimately similar settings

- Choose the right temperature – colours can be washed in cold water. White can usually be washed in warm water while bed linen and pillow cases will need hot water to kill any bacteria. When in doubt use cold water as hot water can potentially shrink clothes.

- Do not overstuff the machine as clothes won't be cleaned as well if you do this.

- Once the load is done, shake the clothes out before hanging them on the clothesline so that they dry easier. You may need to learn how to peg clothes correctly. Or a great tip: hang clothes directly onto a coat-hanger to dry so that they have fewer wrinkles post-drying out on the line.

- Once they are dry, fold them neatly into the basket or iron and put away immediately to minimise creases.

Like all the skills in this book you shouldn't just assume that you know how to do this. Even if you have been encouraged to help with different steps you may never have carried through the whole process from beginning to end.

Knowing how to use a washer and dryer to get your clothes clean is an essential skill, especially if you need to look clean and neat for your job in the future. So make sure you are familiar with all the steps in the laundry process.

2. HOW TO MOW THE LAWN

Operating a lawn mower and keeping it running smoothly is a great skill to learn if you one day plan to have a home that isn't overwhelmed by an out-of-control savannah.

Some tips to keep in mind:

- Wait for your lawn to be dry before moving as cutting wet grass can result in an uneven cut and also clog your mower. Also avoid mowing in the heat of the day as this can damage the grass.

- Ensure the edges have been trimmed first with appropriate equipment such as a Whipper Snipper. This will establish the perimeter of the yard so you can see where you need to mow. The mower will also pick up these clippings.

- Mow only as often as is needed for your grass type. This will vary according to the season, growing conditions and growth pattern of your lawn.

- Change the mowing pattern each time you mow to avoid compacting the soil.

- Keep mower blade sharp for the cleanest cut. Before you mow make sure you clean the yard of any sticks or branches to ensure the life of the mower blades.

- Make sure you understand that operating a lawnmower improperly can cause serious injury including death so you must be mindful of your safety when using one. Always wear hearing and eye protection and tough, closed-toe shoes while mowing.

- Have a responsible adult show you the ropes a few times before giving this a go on your own.

3. HOW TO IRON

Ironing clothes is a task that can seem terrifying and complicated at first but honestly it is simple enough once you have mastered it.

Some tips to keep in mind:

- You will need to understand that different materials require different types of ironing and some actually require special attention. As such, before you begin, clothing will need to be sorted according to material type.

- Delicate fabrics need to be turned inside out before ironing as ironing the surface as cause the fabric to be damaged. This includes: linen, rayon, satin, silk and wool. These should be ironed with **low heat.**

- Other fabrics, namely cotton and polyester, need to be damp prior to ironing as these fabrics should not be ironed dry. You can spritz these with a spray bottle to get them damp. Polyester clothing should be ironed on medium heat and cotton on high heat.

- When ironing shirts, lay the shirt flat on the ironing board. Start by ironing the back of the shirt first and once you have done the back, do the sides of the item.

Next do the sleeves and last but not least do the folded collar to maintain its creases.

- When ironing pants, do so from the waist to the leg,

- Items like buttons should be ironed around, as these are prone to damage.

- An iron is very hot and can cause serious injury to people. Let the iron cool off for at least 10 minutes before putting it away in order to give it adequate time to cool.

- In the event of an accident, a burn will heal faster with proper treatment. Run the burn under cool running water for about 20 minutes.

4. HOW TO CHANGE THE SHEETS

One of life's treats is getting into bed at night with freshly made-up linen. But too often this task isn't done often enough.

Some tips to keep in mind:

- Shower each night before bed. This will help keep the sheets cleaner for longer.

- Bed sheets should be washed at least every other week (once a fortnight) unless you are a night sweater in which case you need to wash your bed sheets weekly. Pillow cases should be done more often and can be easily changed once a week.

- Understand why it's so important to change your bed sheets. Dirt and dust can build up quickly and dust mites can be lurking in our sheets. In addition, we shed a million skin cells every night and when you add oil and sweat to the mix, your sheet's cleanliness can get nasty quite quickly. When you are sick, your bedding will need to be changed more frequently.

- To get this task done on schedule, simply wake up and strip the bed on the day you have planned to wash the sheets. Stripping the bed should only take a few minutes and once they are being laundered, you have no choice but to fit the bed with new sheets. It can feel like a daunting task but in reality it can be quick and simple.

5. HOW TO WASH THE DISHES

There's a chance you may have grown up with a dishwasher and hence never learn the simple skill of how to wash dishes. But it's an important skill to learn, in case you ever need to wash up without the help of a machine.

Some tips to keep in mind:

- Use thick rubber gloves to protect your hands.

- Before you begin scrape any leftover food from the dishes, straight into a bin.

- Plug the drain and fill the sink with hot soapy water, making the water as comfortably hot as possible. The hotter the water, the cleaner your dishes will be.

- Items should be washed in a particular order (usually cleanest to dirtiest):

    o Glasses

    o Cutlery

    o Plates

    o Cook wear (pots and pans)

- You can opt to soak dirtier items at the bottom of the sink as this will make it easier to clean them later on. Scrub and clean each item thoroughly with a sponge or washcloth. You may need extra soap for dirtier items, if any residue remains.

- Rinse items under a warm running tap in the adjacent sink and then drip dry on a drying rack. Otherwise dry it with a clean, dry towel.

- Don't forget to rinse out your brush or sponge after use. If it starts to smell unpleasant it is time to throw it away and get a new one. Also turn your gloves inside out to dry.

6. HOW TO SEW AND MEND

Accidents happen and one day you may get a hole in our pants or lose a button on your shirt. And what will you do then: do you mend the item or toss it straight into the Goodwill pile?

The chances are high that an item can be easily repaired instead of being tossed away. As such, you will need to know how to use a needle and thread to sew up a hole, patch up an item or re-attach a button to a favorite shirt. These skills that are quickly becoming lost in this world of easy come, easy go but they are simple enough to learn.

Here are some sewing basics:

- Have a basic sewing kit, which includes needles, thread, measuring tape, pins and scissors in your home.

- Learn how to thread a needle. You will need to cut twice as much thread as you think you will need. Licking the end can make it easier to guide your thread through the eye of a needle.

- Know how to finish it with a knot. You may need to do a double knot to secure it properly.

- Know how to do some basic stitches. You will need to pierce the wrong side of the fabric – that is, the side people won't be seeing.

This is so the knot ends up on the right side of the garment. You will need to make a knot big enough that it doesn't slip straight through the fabric.

- Generally stitches should be done in a straight line. Sew the edges together in a seam and use short stitch lengths to keep it from breaking open.

- Determine the right stitch you need to use for your garment. Common stitches include: basting stitch, running stitch, backstitch and overcast stitch. Information on how to perform any of these common stitches is freely available online.

- Regardless of the stitch you use, you will need to secure it properly to prevent your work from becoming undone. This can be done by pulling the thread through a loop to create a knot, cinching it at the base of the fabric. For a stronger hold, repeat the process a few times to create two or three small knots.

- If you are a novice who is eager to learn how to sew and mend with more flair, consider learning how to operate a sewing machine. You will need to follow the instructions from the appropriate manual or preferably get a first-hand lesson from someone who has already mastered operating this device.

7. HOW TO UNCLOG

A TOILET OR DRAIN

This is a task no-one is eager to tackle but toilets and drains seem to clog at the most inconvenient times. Fortunately you can clear most blocked things yourself without having to call for a plumber. To master this skill you will need to have a good plunger or homemade drain cleaner made up of hot water, baking soda and vinegar.

Here are the steps to follow:

- First things first. You will need to keep the toilet or drain from overflowing. Therefore if your toilet doesn't flush properly after one flush, don't flush it again - instead turn off the water to the toilet. Similarly, if your sink is refusing to drain now is not the time to fill it with more water.

- Next, make sure you have a large heavy-duty rubber plunger you are use. Avoid small cheap suction-cup types of plungers as these usually do not solve the problem. Your plunger will need to make a tight seal in order to work.

- Insert the plunger into the toilet bowl or over the drain. Your plunger needs to be large enough to completely cover the hole and it needs to be submerged in water in order to work. If you can't get the plunger to make a seal wrap an old towel around the bottom of it to help secure the hold.

- Start pumping the plunger over the hole or drain. Continue to forcefully push and pull until the water begins to drain. Don't give up easily. You will need patience here as it can take 20-25 times before the water begins to drain.

- If this doesn't work you have another option. You can either purchase an enzyme waste removal product. These enzymes will liquefy the waste materials that are blocking your drain. This method will however only work on organic waste and won't help if you have blocked your drain with metal or plastic objects. You will need to follow the instructions on the bottle.

- Alternatively you can make a homemade drain cleaner. Simply add 1 cup of baking soda and 2 cups of vinegar to 2 litres of hot water (slightly hotter than tea you can drink comfortably). The mixture will fizz a lot but that's how you know it is working. Pour the mixture into the toilet or drain and let sit overnight.

- If your toilet or drain is still clogged after performing these options you may have a hard obstruction causing the clog so try using a wire coat hanger or a drain snake to remove it. Twist and move the snake until the water starts to drain.

- If you have tried all of the above and your toilet or drain is still clogged, you may need to admit defeat and call a plumber to do the job as the problem may be buried deep within the pipes. In these instances, it is best to leave the job to a professional.

8. HOW TO SET A TABLE

You have probably sat down to eat dinner with your family countless times but that doesn't mean you have paid attention to or memorised the way a table is properly set. It is up to you to learn this skill!

Here are the instructions to a basic table setting, appropriate for most occasions.

- Placemat first.

- Dinner plate in positioned in the centre of the place setting and everything else is arranged around it.

- The FORK is placed to the left of the plate.

- The KNIFE and SPOON are placed to the right of the plate with the sharp edge of the knife facing the plate. To the right of the knife is the spoon.

- The WATER GLASS is placed above the knife. An additional wine glass, if needed, should be placed on the right side of it, near the corner of the placemat.

- The NAPKIN is to be folded in half and placed beneath the fork.

- If soup is to be served place the BOWL on top of the plate.

- If you require additional utensils such a smaller salad fork, remember this general rule: you should be eating with the utensils from the outside in. In a more formal setting, you start with the utensils on the outside of your plate and work your way closer to the plate until the end of the meal.

9. HOW TO KEEP THE
HOUSE CLEAN

Kids and teens are known for being messy and unorganised but a tidy room and tidy house often equals a tidy mind. This is especially important when you are older. We all feel happier and more productive when we get our possessions in order.

Here are some tips to get your house
looking and staying as clean as possible:

- For starters throw away everything you don't love or need. If it doesn't bring you joy or isn't useful to you now is the time to bin it. Nothing makes you feel more mature than knowing exactly where everything is.

- Your room and workspace doesn't have to perfect but it does help if you understand there is "a place for everything and everything in its place." Don't put things down "just for now" – put it back where it belongs! The rule is simple: *take it out, put it away.*

- Make your bed as soon as you wake up. This one task automatically makes your bedrooms feel tidier.

- Wipe and clear your counters daily.

- Wash the dishes and clean your sink daily. This will prevent your kitchen from looking like a bomb hit it.

- Start the day with a load of laundry. If it's there to be done, just get it done! Iron, fold and put it away promptly too.

- Vacuum at least once a week. Sweep floors ideally once a day.

- Finally every day do something – anything! -to keep your house looking clean. One day it might be cleaning the toilets, the next day it might be mopping or dusting.

If you follow just these steps it will help keep your house looking cleaner for longer.

10. HOW TO DO BASIC HOME IMPROVEMENTS

As an adult, things will sometimes break and items will need your attention at home. When this happens you have a few options: you can either call a repair guy, beg your friends to help, or attend to the job yourself. Given that most repair work is rather costly, this is a great skill to master.

We don't expect anyone to tackle difficult electrical or plumbing work on their own but here are a few simple home improvement tasks that are straight-forward enough to learn.

- Change a lightbulb

- Hang a painting

- Paint a room

- Clear blocked drains or toilets

- Fit insulation

- Put together a flat-pack furniture item

- Steam clean your carpet

While we are on the subject of home improvement, it's pretty much a sign of adulthood when you inherit or buy your first toolbox.

Essential items to keep inside this box include:

- Claw Hammer

- Pliers

- Screwdriver (Flathead and Phillips)

- Adjustable wrench

- Measuring tape

- Level

- Utility Knife

- Electrical Drill

- Flashlight

- Nails

11. HOW TO PICK UP
AFTER YOURSELF

Want to know the quickest way to get the house looking like a mess? It's by not returning things to their place. Test it out and before you know it your house will look like a pigsty. In order to master this simple skill you will need to become vigilant with putting things away when they are done using them.

Some tips to master this skill include:

- Do not allow laundry to accumulate. As soon as it is off the line, ironed and folded, put it away in the cupboard or drawer.

- Put dirty clothes straight into the hamper, not the floor.

- Dirty dishes need to be stacked into the dishwasher or washed.

- Mail and important papers need to be filed away. If you have a bill to pay either pay it immediately or put it with the few that you have scheduled to pay on a particular day.

- Clothing and shoes needs to be returned to the closet.

- Toys and books go straight back into the toy box or bookshelf.

- When you are done using something it needs to be put away where it belongs. Remember the most important rule: a place for everything and everything in its place!

- If you enter a room leave it exactly as you found it (assuming it's neat and tidy – otherwise you need to get it looking back to normal!)

- Consistency is an important part of learning this skill. Cleaning and tidying up after yourself may be boring but it's a necessary task to keep your home and life in order. So the sooner you master this skill, the better!

Outside The Home

12. HOW TO KEEP PLANTS ALIVE

Having plants inside and outside the home are a beautiful addition to your décor but keeping them alive is not always easy. Plants needs light, water, support and nutrients but they also require a bit of know-how to keep them alive.

Some simple tips to keep your plants alive include:

- Try to work out what your particular plant is called. This research will help you find additional information on how to take care of it. Make "right plant, right place" your motto.

- Give your plant the light it needs. Different plants require a different amount of light. Keep them away from very hot, cold or drafty areas in your home. If your plant has paler foliage it could be an indication that it is not getting enough light.

- Pay attention to its soil. You can do this by checking the soil regularly. When the soil looks dry, just stick your finger into it – if it is dry in the first couple of centimetres it is probably time to give the plant more water. If the soil is still wet a few days after your last watering, it means you have overwatered it. You need to let the soil dry out before you water it again. Once a week is usually fine unless they need water earlier.

41

- Make sure your plant is happy. This means you will need to check your plant for any pests and dust build-up.

- Be sure to prune regularly. Remove any dead, brown and yellow leaves and stem as well to allow for new growth.

13. HOW TO PARALLEL PARK

It's amazing how even though all driving tests require this skill, many people with their license still haven't mastered parallel parking. If you have any plans to drive a car in the future, then it's fair to say this skill won't go astray.

This is especially important if you live in the city - you will need to learn how to do this correctly so you don't "accidentally" bump into the hood or bumpers of the other people's cars. If it was part of the driving test, you should know how to do it properly.

Tips on how to master this essential skill include:

- Drive around until you find a spot that looks big enough to accommodate your car. It's best to find a space that is a few feet (or a metre) longer than your car.

- Signal to others with your indicator that you are planning to park here and pull up even to the front car so that your windows are aligned. The tighter the space the closer you will need to get to the other car. Approximately two feet or 60 centimetres is best.

- Stop here and turn your wheel all the way to the right, creating a 45 degree angle. Once this is done, check your rear view mirrors again and turn around, looking out the back of your car.

- Now you can begin backing into the spot. Release the brakes and slowly begin turning and backing into the spot. Straighten out as you finish pulling in. If you have done this correctly you will be tucked in nicely in a parallel park.

- If you're not confident about parking you can ask a passenger to get out and help guide you into the spot. Alternatively if you don't feel comfortable trying it out on a busy road, test practice your skills in an empty parking lot. You can even bring along some chairs to create your designated parking space and have a friend guide you through the process. Take your time and don't rush – eventually practice will make perfect.

14. HOW TO BUILD A CAMPFIRE

While this is not a skill you will need to demonstrate on a daily basis, it definitely makes a person feel confident just knowing they have mastered this essential survival skill. Fire is indeed one of our most important elements and helps provide warmth, light and energy. They are also fun to build on camping trips or whenever else it might be handy!

Here are some useful tips to building a campfire:

- Note that fires can only be built in a designated fire rings, grills, fireplaces or areas. Always make sure fires are permitted before you build one.

- To burn a successful fire you will need:
    - Tinder which includes small twigs, dry leaves and paper.
    - Kindling which consists of small sticks.
    - Firewood which is any larger piece of chopped wood that will keep your fire going.

- The easiest and most popular method is the tepee style campfire. Make a loose pile of tinder and build a tepee with the kindling around the tinder.

- Light the tinder with a match of lighter. Then blow gently at the base of the fire which will help increase the intensity of the flame. Fires need a lot of oxygen to keep it going.

- As the fire grows, feed it with branches and eventually, once the fire is strong, you can add larger logs a few at a time as needed.

- Put out the fire by letting the wood burn out, dousing it with water, or covering it with sand or dirt. Be sure it is completely out and cold before leaving the area.

15. HOW TO ORDER AT A RESTAURANT

Even if you have eaten at a restaurant numerous times do not just assume you know how to order. There's a good chance you have never ordered for yourself, when in the company of parents or other adults.

Here are some etiquette rules that should be followed when ordering at a restaurant:

- Look the waiter or waitress in the eye when you are ordering.

- Make sure to be polite and communicate your request clearly and politely. If you have invited a guest out let him or her order first.

- Remember to say thank you.

- It's important to have made up your mind by the time the waiter or waitress comes to take your order. If you need more time to decide, it is okay to request a few more minutes to decide.

- Keep in mind that the restaurant won't always allow for separate payments so be prepared to pull out a calculator and contribute your share of payment at the end of the meal when the bill arrives.

- It is considered rude form to put your elbows on the table. Also do not put your cell phone, keys or purse on the table. It not only distracts you but your other dining companions.

- Remember to take your napkin and place it in your lap. If you excuse yourself to go to the bathroom, leave the napkin on your chair.

- When you finish with the meal, neatly place the napkin on the left side of your plate on the table. Also place your utensils on the plate (the knife and fork together at the 10:20 position) when you are finished with your meal. This is silent restaurant code that you have finished eating.

- Finally don't yell at your waiter for the bill. The proper technique is to try and make eye contact but if that doesn't work, it is fine to put up your right hand with your index finer slightly raised to get their attention.

16. HOW TO TAKE PUBLIC TRANSPORTATION

While it would be great to have a car or personal chauffeur to transport us whenever we need to go, the fact of the matter is sometimes it's easier or necessary to take a bus, train or ferry instead. Do not assume you will necessarily know how to do this!

To master this skill,

here's what you need to know:

- Find out the bus routes and train and ferry timetable for your city or town. These are often available online or alternatively you can contact your local bus, train or ferry depot.

- Purchase a ticket – often these can be purchased as a weekly or multi-trip pass. There are also discounts usually available for students or those with a disability. .

- Decide which is your closest bus, ferry or train-stop. You will need to check both pickup and return times specific for this particular stop.

- Make sure your mode of public transportation is going in the right direction! You can do this by always double-checking with the driver or staff first to confirm this is the correct route.

- If you are issued a ticket, make sure you put it in a safe place in case an inspector asks to check it later.

- Before you exit the bus, train or ferry, double check where you were sitting to make sure you left nothing behind and be sure to thank the driver before leaving.

- If you make a mistake and get off at the wrong stop, don't panic! Be prepared to ask for help so you can find the correct route home.

- Some basic etiquette rules when taking public transport:

  - Always let the passengers exit first

  - Do not block the doors

  - Have your card or money ready before you enter the bus

  - Always offer your seat to a pregnant or elderly person, or someone with special needs.

  - Do not take up more than one seat for yourself. Place your bag on your lap.

  - Use headphones if you are listening to music

  - Refrain from having loud conversations, whether it's with or without your phone

  - Don't drink or eat food when travelling on public transport

  - Cover your mouth if you have to sneeze or cough

  - Respect other people's personal space and privacy

17. HOW TO BE A RESPECTFUL HOUSE GUEST

You never know when you might need to accept the hospitality of a friend or family member and in these instances it is important that you know the proper etiquette of being a gracious house guest.

Some important things for house guests to remember:

1. **Provide your host with specific dates that you will be coming**

   Don't keep your visit open-ended because it's extremely rude to overstay your welcome. Be respectful with the time you choose to stay – if your host is busy during your visit then you may need stay with someone else for the second part of your trip. Arrive when you say you will arrive and leave when you say you will leave.

2. **Pack well**

   Bring just enough clothing and items for the duration of your visit.

3. It's absolutely essential that you bring a thank you gift

Your gift doesn't have to be expensive but it is important to be caring and thoughtful. Appropriate gift ideas include: flowers, a box of chocolates, candles, an appreciative thank you card, taking the family out to dinner or homemade treats.

4. Follow the house rules

This means you may need to ask or clarify what they are. If your host does not allow shoes inside the house, then don't wear shoes inside the house. If they have quiet time after nine p.m., then make sure you too after quiet after this time. Be mindful of internet and TV usage and always ask first before using something.

5. Don't expect your host to do everything for you

Remember they are doing you a favor by letting you stay! Offer to help out with the chores like washing the dishes, laundry, preparing meals and taking out the trash. Your host is also not a babysitter or tour guide. Be prepared to plan your own outings and communicate your comings and goings from their home. Don't ever leave their home without telling them first where you have gone!

6. **Keep your guest area tidy**

This means doing common sense things like making your bed, cleaning up after any mess you make and keeping your belongings packed up neatly.

7. **Offer to contribute**

Whether you realise or not, your presence may result in an additional cost to your host so be prepared to contribute to groceries or replace things you have used.

18. HOW TO GET FROM A TO B

Having a sense of direction comes more naturally to some people than others, but it is an important skill to master to confidently get from A to B. Thankfully we don't need to rely on a street directory anymore when a GPS device or an app on your phone now often does the job even better now.

There is no excuse anymore for getting completely lost just because you missed one turn. If this happens you need to be able to take out a map or use a GPS to collect your bearings and find out where your destination is. You need to have some foresight to work out how to connect the dots from A to B.

Some tips for when you don't have a map or compass on you and don't want to get lost in the unknown:

- Ask others for help if anyone is around.

- If you are alone in the wilderness remember this: the sun rises in the east and sets in the west. So use the sun as your guide. If it's morning the sun will be rising in the east and in the afternoon it will be roughly setting in the west so you can use these facts to figure out the approximate directions of north and south as well.

- At night locate the North Star (Polaris) in the sky. The North Star is the last star in the Little Dipper. If you draw an imaginary line straight down from the North Star to the ground, you can work out where true north is and use it to guide yourself.

Remember just because you have a driver's license doesn't mean you necessarily have good navigational skills. If you need to travel for work or school, it's important to practice this skill until you feel confident enough to get from A to B, even in an unfamiliar city.

19. HOW TO TAKE CARE OF A CAR

There's a good chance that you will aspire to drive and own your own set of wheels one day but along with skill comes a new set of responsibilities. Cars are expensive machines that need to be taken care of well and it's vital that you know some basic auto-maintenance skills in order to stay safe and properly operate this costly possession.

Unfortunately there is not nearly enough space in this book to describe in detail the steps required to accomplish these skills (we will leave the actual learning up to you!).

Here are a few basic auto-maintenance skills you should be looking to master:

- How to change a tire and where to find the jack and spare tire.

- How to jumpstart a car and where to get jumper cables (make sure you have some in the car in case of an emergency).

- How to check the oil level and change the oil and how often to do it.

- How to check the tire pressure and how to fill it to the appropriate pressure

- How to pump gas with the right fuel.

- The importance of regular maintenance (which can save and prevent more costly repair bills later on).

- Who to call in chance of an auto emergency.

You do not need to know everything but the above list not only covers the basic skills, it also helps build confidence. Please note: just watching someone do it once is not enough for anyone to learn this skill. You will need to do it yourself in order to learn so make sure you are guided through this exercise and try it out yourself. Don't wait until an emergency arises.

Also, it is important that you know which vehicle is best for you to buy, based on performance and safety ratings, which vehicles they should avoid, and which holds the most resale value.

20. HOW TO PUMP GAS

We decided to feature this skill separate from the general auto-maintenance category as it is so imperative you know how to do this correctly. When you first learn to drive, you might find that the car is magically always filled with gas. Parents have a tendency to fill the tank themselves and some even do so after the teen has purchased his or her car so it's important they master this skill.

Here are the rules to follow:

- Understand that fuel vapours are extremely flammable so make sure to never smoke or use a lighter in the presence of gas and put away your cell phone first (cell phone usage at a fuel station is generally not recommended as cell static has been linked to several gas station flare-ups.)

- Pull up to the correct side of the fuel pump. You can determine which side of the car your gas tank is located by looking on the gas indicator on your dashboard. It will usually have a small arrow pointing to the gas tank side of your car.

- Turn your car off first as it's unsafe to pump fuel into your car while it is still running.

- Determine which fuel your car requires – some cars run on diesel or ethanol. This is absolutely important as using the wrong fuel can have detrimental effects on your vehicle and cause major mechanical problems.

- Insert the nozzle into the fuel tank and depress the handle of the pump to lock it into place. You can then squeeze the fuel pump handle and allow the fuel to flow into the tank. It should automatically shut off when the tank is full.

- Replace your fuel cap and tighten until you hear it click or it stops. If it doesn't seal properly the engine light may illuminate noting something is amiss.

- Pay for your fuel – this sometimes will need to be done before you begin pumping gas.

STAYING ALIVE

21. HOW TO COOK SOMETHING THAT DOESN'T COME IN A BOX

Cooking is one of those skills that never go unnoticed. It is a useful skill to master, not only because food is essential to life but also because cooking fresh food with fresh ingredients equal GOOD HEALTH (and health is the greatest wealth we can have)

At some point you will need to learn that you cannot survive and function on junk food alone. That's because in the long run, eating crap will make you FEEL like crap. Cooking at home, on the other hand, generally saves both time and money, and the ingredients and portion sizes can be controlled by YOU. You buy the ingredients so you control what is going on your plate!

Please note however when I say cook I DO NOT mean microwaving a frozen meal or pouring boiling water onto packaged noodles. Instead I mean being able to prepare quick, basic and nutritious meals.

Here are some basic skills you should master:

- Scramble eggs
- Cook Plain Rice
- Cook Plain Pasta
- Roast a Chicken

- Marinade or Season Meat

- Grill a Steak or Meat

- Steam Vegetables

- Put together a Salad

- Bake a Cake

  (Note: homemade banana bread will always be healthier than any processed, store-bought confectionary).

You will also need to understand the different methods of cooking:

- Boiling

- Frying

- Sautéing

- Roasting

- Grilling/Barbequing

- Broiling

Just remember knowing how to cook can give you a real sense of freedom and independence. When you master this skill, you have the personal satisfaction of knowing you can nourish your body well and literally make good choices yourself.

Thankfully the internet is filled with countless recipes for home cooking and step-by-step instructions so please feel to check these out and practice your cooking skills until you feel confident enough to do it on your own.

5 Basic Meals That Are Delicious and Simple to Master

- Fried chicken and mashed potatoes

- Minestrone soup

- Spaghetti Bolognaise

- Risotto with seafood or chicken

- Stir-fry with vegetables

22. HOW TO KNOW WHEN
YOU ARE SICK

Over the course of our lifetime we all occasionally get sick. When we're young, it is nice because we still have our parents to comfort and take care of us but at some point you will need to do that for yourself. Have you learned to recognise when you are not well?

In order to master this skill you will need to make sure you know how to self-diagnose simple illnesses.

Other things you should know how to do:

- Check your own temperature (if you have a fever of 100 F or 38 C, you are sick enough to stay home!)

- Know how to treat a cold or flu

- Know when to go to the doctor

- Know when to rest in bed versus go to work or school

  o Hint: stay at home if you have a fever, diarrhoea, strange rash or uncontrollable coughing

- Know which over-the-counter medications to take for which symptoms

- Know the importance of having a regular medical check-ups, including pap smears and breast checks for women and prostrate checks for men

- Understand the importance of refraining from smoking, limiting alcohol and eating well to maintain good health

- Understand the importance of physical exercise –aim to be active for 30 minutes on most or all days.

23. HOW TO PERFORM CPR

CPR is an amazing skill that can save a person's life but the vast majority of people don't know what to do if someone is experiencing a cardiac emergency.

While it is highly recommended that you take a certified CPR class (Why? Because knowing how to perform CPR can save the life of a loved one someday) here are the basic facts you need to know if you ever face a situation where someone requires immediate respiratory care.

BEFORE YOU START

Check for responsiveness by asking if the victim is okay in a loud, clear voice. If there is no response, call emergency services immediately.

For Adults And Children 9 Years And Older (Hands Only Technique If You Are Not Trained In CPR):

1. Lay the patient on their back and kneel next to their neck and shoulders.

2. Place the heel of one hand on the centre of the patient's chest (exactly between their nipples).

Then place the heel of your other hand over the first and lace your fingers together.

3.   Position your body directly over your hands, keeping your elbows straight and your shoulders aligned directly over your hands

4.   Begin compressions by pressing down around 2 inches (5 centimetres) and do so in a relatively steady and fast rhythm (about 100 beats per minutes). Some professionals recommend doing it to the beat of the chorus of Staying Alive by the Bee Gees.

5.   The American Heart Association no longer consider rescue breaths necessary for CPR as chest compressions are considered to be more important. If you have never done CPR before please stick with only chest compressions.

6.   Continue CPR until emergency services arrive, someone else takes over for you, you are too exhausted to continue or until signs of life return.

For Younger Children And Infants

1.   Tilt the head back slightly and lift the chin to open the airway and check for breathing

2.   If there is no breathing you will need to pinch the nose shut and make a complete seal over the mouth for a child. For an infant make a complete seal over the mouth and nose.

3. Blow in for a second so the chest visibly rises. Repeat once.

4. Then give 30 chest impressions just below the nipples. Push with 1 or 2 hands about 2 inches (5 centimetres) deep. With an infant push with 2-3 fingers about 1.5 inches (3 centimetres) deep. The rate of compressions is still at least 100 times per minutes.

5. Repeat steps 3 and 4 until emergency services arrive, someone else takes over or breathing resumes.

6. Even if the infant or young child seems fine by the time help arrives, a doctor will still need to check him or her to make sure he or she hasn't sustained any internal injuries.

24. HOW TO SWIM

The statistics on death by drowning
are truly terrifying

- Drowning is the third leading cause of unintentional death worldwide and accounts for 7% of all injury-related deaths

- Every day approximately 10 people drown in the U.S.

- About one in five fatal drowning victims are children younger than 14

- Drowning is also a silent killer—most young children who drowned in pools were out of sight for less than five minutes, and in the care of one or both parents at the time

- If a parent does not know how to swim, there is only a 13 percent chance that a child in that household will learn how to swim.

The fact is drowning is a major worldwide public health issue and if you don't know how to swim yet, you need to seriously consider learning how to do so. There are a number of emergency situations where you might need to swim in order to survive or help someone else in the water.

Swimming can seem intimidating if you have never learned to do it but it is also a skill that can be acquired quickly if you have the courage and persistence to master it.

To learn how to swim, you will need to conquer the following skills:

- Let go of your fear and get comfortable in the water.

- Learn how to float

- Remember not to panic – if you find yourself in deep water you can always resort to floating until you regain your composure

- Practice kicking your legs and learn how to tread water

- Learn how to do some simple strokes like freestyle (American crawl) or backstroke

- If you are swimming in the ocean, you may get caught in a riptide. Do not panic if this happens. Instead swim sideways in a parallel line to the shore. Alternatively if you get caught in a river current, swim diagonally to the shore.

- Finally take lessons with a certified swim school until you have mastered the most important strokes. Alternatively you can use a floatation device until you feel comfortable enough to swim on your own in the water

25. HOW TO PERFORM THE HEIMLICH MANEUVER

Choking is a situation no one wants to find him or herself faced with but given that a choking victim can't speak or breathe, mastering this skill can make a real difference between life and death in some instances. Choking will often be sudden and knowing how to do the Heimlich Maneuver properly can save someone's life. Keep in mind there are a few different manoeuvres you can use on others, on yourself, and on small children.

Here are the steps you are perform the Heimlich manoeuvre on a choking victim:

1. Stand behind the victim. From behind, wrap your arms around the victim's waist.

2. Make a fist with your dominant hand and place your thumb side of your fist against the victim's upper abdomen. This is below the ribcage but above the belly button.

3. Grab your fist with your other hand and press hard into their upper abdomen area with a quick upward thrust. Pull inward and upward using good force.

4. Repeat this action until the object is dislodged.

5. Do not slap the victim back as this can make matter worse.

When the victim is a child follow these steps:

1. Lay the child down on the floor, face up and kneel at their feet or hold an infant on your lap facing away from you.

2. Place the middle and index fingers of both your hands below his or her rib cage. Press into the victim's upper abdomen with a quick, gentle upward thrust.

3. Repeat until the object has been expelled.

If you are choking yourself you can follow these steps to save yourself from choking:

1. Make a first and place the thumb side of your fist against your upper abdomen.

2. Grab your fist with your other hand and press into your upper abdomen with a quick upward thrust.

3. Repeat until the object is expelled.

4. Alternatively you can leave other a fixed object like a table edge, railing or chair and press your upper abdomen against the edge to produce a quick upward thrust. Repeat until the object is expelled.

Call emergency services immediately and remain with the victim constantly as they may require CPR if the object is not cleared with these steps. Make sure the victim also sees a doctor after the rescue to make sure all is fine with him or her.

26. HOW TO PRACTISE
GOOD DENTAL HYGIENE

We all know we are supposed to do it and there's a good chance your parents have tried to drum in the importance of dental hygiene into you countless times. But this information doesn't always sink in. At some point however you will need to know how to pick up that toothbrush and use it without being yelled at to do so.

The basic things you will need to know include:

- Teeth must be brushed for 2 minutes using a proper technique, with an equal amount of time (30 seconds) spent on each quadrant of the mouth

- All surfaces of their teeth must be brushed – including the sides and chewing surface on the top

- Teeth are to be brushed twice a day

- Floss teeth once a day, making sure to also floss the teeth at the back of the mouth

- Rinse mouth with mouthwash after you brush and floss your teeth for 30 seconds

- Don't forget to clean your tongue too with a toothbrush in circular motions

- Change your toothbrush as soon as it starts to look tatty (usually every three months)

- Finally visit your dentist regularly for check-ups and cleanings. A professional cleaning will remove all the built-up plaque and tartar on your teeth that you are not able to remove with brushing and flossing. Every six months is most ideal.

27. HOW TO GROCERY SHOP

Have you ever joined your parents when they go out to do their grocery shopping? Do you know how to navigate a supermarket on your own? If not, it is up to you to learn this skill.

Important points you need to remember:

- Start small. Even when you are young, it is fine to get a short list and find five things while your parents are supervising you in a supermarket.

- It helps to have a shopping list and a planned weekly menu. There is a better chance you will purchase the right things if you know exactly you need for the week.

- Set a budget for the shopping expedition. It is easier to be mindful of the purchases you make when you have a budget you need to stick to.

- Don't go shopping for groceries when you are hungry. When you are hungry you are more tempted to buy all sorts of junk.

- Buy in bulk when it makes sense to do so.

- Use coupons or purchase items on special in order to save money and stick to your budget. But only buy things if they are items you will use.

- Be mindful at the register and make sure to check your receipt before leaving the store to catch any incorrectly priced items.

- Buy fruits and vegetables when they are in season as they will be cheaper then. You will generally want to pick firm produces that isn't bruised.

- Try to purchase whole, unprocessed foods as these are healthier options. Avoid the junk food aisles which are usually at the centre of the store. If you can avoid it, you won't be tempted to buy it.

- If an item is on sale but the store has run of the stock remember to ask for a rain check (you will receive the item at the advertised price when it comes back in stock).

28. HOW TO PERFORM BASIC FIRST AID

Accidents can happen at any time and being equipped with the knowledge of how to perform basic first aid in such an emergency is definitely a confidence booster.

This book has covered CPR and Heimlich Manoeuvre in separate tips but there are other first aid skills that will bring you peace of mind and confidence. Because you never know...sometimes there's no time to wait for a doctor. One day someone you care about or even YOU might get hurt and it will be up to you to treat the wound. In such instances you need to know how to do it right.

BASIC FIRST AID SKILLS:

1. Know how to stop heavy bleeding

Do this by putting pressure on the wound with ideally a sterile cloth and raising the wound above the heart to help slow down bleeding. Do not remove the pressure for any reason until medical help arrives. When the bleeding has stopped, you need to clean and disinfect the wound to avoid infections (warm water is fine if you don't have a disinfectant on hand).

Note: For a nosebleed do not make the victim raise their head or lie down. Instead pinch the nostrils closed for around ten minutes to allow the broken vein to close.

2. Know how to treat shock

Have the victim lie on their back with their feet elevated. Cover them with a blanket to keep them warm.

3. Know how to treat and dress a burn

Soak the wound under cool water for at least five minutes or until pain stops. Do not use ice or ice water as it can cause tissue damage. Take ibuprofen for pain relief and apply a soothing cream that contains aloe Vera. If the burn appears serious and larger than 3 inches in diameter, please seek medical assistance.

4. Recognize the warning signs of a concussion

See medical attention immediately if you experience any of these symptoms following a blow or jolt to the head: loss of consciousness, memory loss, headache, vomiting, seizure or feeling dazed or confused.

5. Recognize the warning signs of a stroke

The National Stroke Foundation recommends the F.A.S.T test as the quickest and easiest way to remember the most common signs of a stroke.

F = FACE

Check their face. Has their mouth drooped? Ask "show me your teeth."

A = ARMS

Ask the person to close their eyes and raise their arms. Can they lift both arms?

S = SPEECH

Ask them to repeat a simple sentence. Is their speech slurred? Do they understand you?

T = TIME

If you see any of these signs call emergency straight away.

29. HOW TO KEEP YOURSELF CLEAN

Keeping your body clean is an important part of keeping yourself healthy. It also helps you to feel good about yourself. We all feel better when we don't smell bad or feel dirty! If you want to go out into the world and form good relationships with others, personal hygiene is without a doubt an important skill to master. Poor personal hygiene can have significant implications on job success and can alienate others.

Most important things to remember:

CLOTHING

- You need to change your underwear and socks DAILY.

- Other clothes need to be laundered regularly as they can get stained, dirty and stinky even after one wear.

BODY

- Shower regularly, and wash all areas well with soap, including your feet.

- Once you hit puberty daily use of an ANTI-PERSPIRANT DEODORANT is an absolute must.

- Shave facial hair regularly (for boys) and legs and underarms (for girls) unless you have opted for a different hair removal plan.

HAIR

- Wash regularly with shampoo (and conditioner if you have long hair) as your hair follicles produce oil and your scalp has sweat glands and dead skin cells. This all together equals greasy, dirty hair if you don't wash it regularly.

- Comb or brush hair daily to keep it neat and free from knots. If you have long hair, you may choose to tie it back with a hair tie to keep it neat.

TEETH

- Brush your teeth twice daily – before breakfast and before you go to bed.

GENERAL CLEANLINESS

- Hand washing is important as most infections are caught when we transfer germs from our hands to our mouth.

- You should wash your hands thoroughly (for at least 20 seconds or sing "Twinkle, Twinkle Little Star") with soap after:

  - going to the toilet
  - preparing and/or eating food
  - handling animals
  - being in the company of someone sick or unwell

- Don't forget to flush toilet after use.
- Don't forget to trim your fingernails and toenails regularly.

30. HOW TO USE CONTRACEPTION

I know this is a sensitive topic that not every parent is comfortable discussing with their kids but this is a must-have skill for all teens and adults to master, especially if you want to avoid an unwanted pregnancy and STDs.

Things you will need to know:

- Your Contraception Options – like condoms, birth control pills, diaphragms, IUDs and emergency options like the morning-after pill

- How to Take The Pill Properly – birth control pills suppress ovulation but they need to be taken every day

- You need to know the most effective way to prevent pregnancy and STDs is abstinence

- Being careless with contraception results in close to half of all unplanned pregnancies

If you don't feel comfortable speaking to your parents about any of this information, your local Planned Parenthood can help or you can simply do your own research. The information is freely available on the Internet and in this instance knowledge is power. Using contraception can prevent your life taking a surprise turn down a road you aren't ready yet to take.

31. HOW TO DEAL WITH AN
EMERGENCY SITUATION

When faced with an emergency our first instinct is to call 911 but there will be times in your life when there's no time to think. Even before or after that call is made, you will need to jump to your feet and DO SOMETHING.

This tip covers non-medical emergencies and it is imperative that you know what to do in such a situation. Always call 911 at the first opportune moment if required or in doubt.

GREASE FIRE

Turn off heat. Put something on top of the pot to remove its oxygen source (ideally a metal lid as glass will shatter). If the grease fire persists and it's small, throw baking soda on it to cut oxygen supply. NEVER throw water onto a grease fire as oil and water don't mix.

NATURAL DISASTERS

Make sure you have a disaster plan if you live in a disaster-prone area. Listen to emergency radio if you suspect there is a natural disaster on its way.

In the case of a tornado, if you are indoors seek shelter in the lowest building level, such as the basement. Stay away from windows, doors and corners of the building. If you are driving and cannot get to shelter, get out of the vehicle and lay face-down in a ditch with your hands over your head, away from the vehicle. Research the internet for what to do in other natural disasters.

INTRODER

If you are faced with a situation of having an intruder in your home, your first priority is your safety. Do not approach the intruder. Make noise to alert the intruder that someone is at home. Your best option is to hide, call the police, give your location and stay on the phone until the police get there.

If you are confronted put your hands up, avoid eye contact and don't try to protect your things as your life is more valuable than any possession. Escaping is a better option than staying to fight so always look for a chance to escape.

POWER OUTAGE

Only open fridge and freezer doors when absolutely necessary. Take care when using candles for light (ideally have some torches stored in your top kitchen drawer for emergencies).

Other tips:

- Don't panic. Remain calm. Take a deep breath and count to 10.

- Check for danger. Protect yourself and others from the hazard.

- Make sure you and your family has a planned and practiced escape route from your home. You should all know the fastest and safest way out of the house and know where you plan to meet in case of an emergency.

- It also helps to have a CODE WORD that signifies danger or a need for urgent help. For example, you could use an unusual name like Barry. So when you hear "Barry can't come over" or "Barry says hello" in an unusual context, then the alarm bells may start ringing earlier for you than later.

32. HOW TO DEFEND YOURSELF

Self-defence is one of those skills that we all would love to master but many never follow up on their desire to learn it. Learning self-defence can however be necessary in protecting our well-bring and that of our loved ones. Not that we want to have to test out this skill but in the event that it is required, it is better to exercise some moves that could equal the preservation of life and limb. After all, it is better to know how to defend oneself and never need to, than need to and not know how to.

Some tips to keep you safe include:

- Always be aware of your surroundings. Look where you are going.

- Maintain a personal comfort zone. Don't allow a potentially hostile stranger to get closer than 5 feet to you without permission.

- Watch your drink – yes, someone can slip in a knock-out dug into your glass when you are not looking.

- Be car smart. Have your keys in your hand before you leave the building. Wait until you are close to your car to unlock it. Never walk to your car alone – ask someone to walk with you if no one else is leaving.

- Learn some self-defence moves. Some ideas include:

  - Don't try to beat a wrist hold by pulling away you're your attacker. Instead rotate your wrist so your thumb lines up with where your attacker's thumb meets his fingers and jerk sharply by bending your arm at the elbow.

  - Kick the sole of your foot at the attacker's knees. The knee is nearly impossible to block.

  - Target your attacker's nose with an upwards palm strike.

  - You can also head-butt your attacker, poke them in the eye, yank their ears or kick them in the groin.

  - Scream – as this can distract an attacker and also works as a signal for help

  - Run away if you can to get away from danger

- Don't try to win! The goal is to put up just enough fight to help you escape from the attack and leave the scene.

- Don't struggle if it could be fatal. If they have a dangerous weapon, struggling could cost you your life.

- Don't be relocated – do whatever you have to do to prevent getting taken to a second location.

- Carrying pepper spray or mace is a good start to self-defence preparedness (unless it is prohibited in your state or country)

33. HOW KNOW TO EAT RIGHT

Teenagers are notoriously famous for eating crap – burgers, French fries, chocolate and chips. This may be fine in moderation but no one can get away with eating rubbish all the time without it having some consequence on their body. Here's the truth: your body is the only home you have to live, so you need to nurture it, honor it, love it and respect it. If you don't do that, whatever you eat in private you will wear in public.

No matter what your age you should never stop taking your health and fitness for granted. Your body is a reflection of your lifestyle. This means understanding that when you clean up your diet and exercise regularly, your weight will take care of itself. You don't have to eat less; you just have to eat right.

To eat well, consider the following tips:

- Drink plenty of water

- Eat plenty of fruit and vegetables

- Choose healthy carbs

- Eat lean protein

- Cut back on sugar

- Know the difference between good fat and bad fat

- Limit processed or fast foods

- Moderation is key

- Don't skip breakfast

Remember being healthy and fit is not a fad or a trend; instead it's a lifestyle choice and something you do for yourself because it makes you feel good. Your health is your greatest wealth and as Ann Wigmore so wisely noted:

"The food you eat can be either the safest and most powerful form of medicine or the slowest form of poison."

YOU NEED MONEY

TO SURVIVE

34. HOW TO FIND A JOB

While the goal of education is primarily to educate children about the world and to fill them with important knowledge, you will ultimately need to be prepared to go out into the workforce and become productive, self-sufficient members of society once your schooling is done.

To do this you will need to master these important skills:

- Identify what you are interested in and passionate about

- Know what skills you are good at and what gifts and talents you have that help you excel

- How to apply for a job and write a resume and cover letter.

- Make sure you apply for a role where you have the adequate skills

- Understand the interview process and what is expected of you

- Understand employment contracts and how to negotiate the terms if required

- It's a numbers game. Apply for lots of jobs with enthusiasm.

35. HOW TO KEEP A JOB

So you have finally found a job. Congratulations! Now you just need to know and understand the expectations of a workplace so you can become an intelligent, productive, hard-working and ethical employee or employer.

To do this you will need to understand:

- That the rules of the workforce are quite different from the confines of a high school or college.

- You will need to come in on time, be punctual, take reasonable breaks and not leave early.

- You need to be dressed presentably. Know what the dress code and expectations are. It is better to be slightly over-dressed than under-dressed.

- If you don't have an answer to a question, it is okay to ask for help.

- Attend to top-priority tasks first.

- Demonstrate good communication, organisational and problem-solving skills.

- Be able to work independently or as part of a team.

- Show enthusiasm and be self-motivated.

- Take initiative and be assertive when it's appropriate.

36. HOW TO BUDGET AND KEEP TRACK OF YOUR SPENDING

Whether you are headed for college or a job straight out of school, a cornerstone of responsible adulthood is being able to manage your own money to pay for rent, bills and any extras which include gas, clothing, insurance, entertainment and food.

You will need to learn how to keep track of your spending. You need to know how to budget your money so you have enough left over at the end of each month.

To do this successfully here are some points to keep in mind:

- You need to understand that you can only buy something if you can afford it.

- There are dozens if not hundreds of software programs available that can help you keep track of your spending.

- Write down your income and expenses. Be aware of where your money goes and how much you need to cover your lifestyle. Make adjustments or sacrifices when required.

- Track all your expenditures, even the little things, because they sometimes really add up.

- Identify your key financial priorities and your biggest money-wasters.

- If you are a low-income earner or budgeting for the first time, it may seem tough but it is a necessary step in order to move to the next stage of financial planning – which is learning to save.

37. HOW TO SAVE MONEY
AND SHOP FRUGALLY

Having good money-management habits modelled for you by your parents gives you a good head-start to survive and master this skill. But don't worry if that didn't happen. You can still learn this skill by having the opportunity to earn money and being encouraged to save a portion of that income. You will also need to know what is worth spending your money on, how to save, and how to invest it too, if you would like to see your money grow.

Some tips to keep in mind when learning to save and shop frugally:

- You should know the difference between spending and investing.

- You should put aside at least 10% of your income for a rainy day, or so you can eventually make a large purchase or down-payment on a home.

- You should know how to shop wisely using coupons and compare prices per unit.

- You should think about ways to increase your earnings as that equals more money in the kitty every month.

- You should know the difference between being cheap and frugal. Being cheap is about spending less; being frugal is about prioritising your spending so that you can have more of the things you really care about.

- Don't buy anything you don't really need, even if it's on sale or has its price slashed dramatically.

- Listen to the wise words of one of the world's richest men, Warren Buffet: "Do not save what is left after spending but spend what is left after saving." The best way to build your savings is by spending less each month.

- It's not efficient to scrimp so much that you are miserable. Aim to find a reasonable, comfortable balance in life.

38. HOW TO USE A CREDIT CARD

This skill is listed separately from learning to save and budget because it has the potential to literally ruin young lives even before you get started. As soon as you are old enough, you can be sure that the offers to get a "free" credit card will start rolling in and you may feel tempted by the idea of free money.

Except of course it isn't free money. You will absolutely need to understand how to use a credit card correctly (or ideally how to avoid using it at all).

Consider the following must-know tips:

- Interest rates are insanely high on credit cards. This means that the balance needs to be paid off IN FULL at the end of each month or you will be charged a hefty interest fee.

- If you still aren't convinced just how hefty these fees are, calculate an example on your own.

- Credit cards ARE NOT for impulse buying. If you must have one then you need to know how to use it responsibly (by paying it out in full each month or saving it for emergency use ONLY). You need to explicitly understand what it is and isn't appropriate to be used for.

- You also need to learn how to resist temptation and how not to succumb to impulse or irresponsible purchases.

By the time you leave home, you MUST understand the relationship between credit and real money! If you can't cover the payments in full it can lead to a lot of heartache and financial loss. This is somehow you will want to avoid, so please ensure you master this skill before it is too late.

39. HOW TO MANAGE TIME AND FOLLOW A SCHEDULE

Effectively managing time is a skill that so many desire but few people have. We all wish there was more time in the day, or at very least that we knew how to manage this time more wisely.

Children can thankfully be taught from a very young age how to follow a schedule. Their mornings will usually follow a simple routine – such as wake up, make the bed, have breakfast, use bathroom and brush teeth. Our schedules become a lot more complicated though as we become older, as our time table must take into account our work or schooling, assignments and other commitments.

Some tips on how to manage your time better:

- If you always need an adult to remind you to do your homework or carry out a chore THEY NEED TO STOP THAT BEHAVIOUR NOW. They are only encouraging you to be lazy. You need to held accountable for your own actions and learn how to manage you time more wisely on their own. Life will naturally offer consequences for tasks not completed.

- Once upon a time, people depended on a watch and wall calendar to keep them on time and organised.

Nowadays we have alarms, alerts and apps on our cell phones to keep us in check. So there's no reason to be lazy or late. You absolutely MUST know how to wake yourself up every day. Do not depend on others to wake you!

- Remember to complete your important tasks first (this is called PRIORITISING), know your deadlines and get an early start on things.

- Create a daily plan and use that calendar!

- Block out any distractions, eliminate time-wasters and don't fuss about the unimportant details.

You also need to know being busy is NOT the same as being productive. Not convinced? Then read this excerpt from my book "LIGHTBULB MOMENTS: 50 AHA! MOMENTS TO TRANSFORM YOUR LIFE" which highlights the difference between the two.

- For starters productive people have a mission for their life and few priorities while busy people have lots on their plate with many priorities. Busy people always jump to say yes whereas productive people are slow to jump and they think a lot before they agree to do something. They want to make sure it is aligned with their long term goals.

- Busy people are always moving where productive people think before they act. Busy people complain about how much they are doing whereas productive people don't need to talk about it.

They let their results prove or show everything. Productive people make time for what is important while busy people don't have time for anything. Productive people are focused and instead of just talking about how they can make a change, they MAKE those changes happen.

- Being busy is often an excuse to not get the important things done. People use it to justify why they are late, why they can't do something, and ironically why they are getting so little done.

- Being busy is when you fill up time with tasks rather than prioritising the important stuff. It's when you work without a system and tackle random tasks without giving thought to urgency. It's when you spend a lot of time doing things that don't really matter. You think "doing" something and keeping yourself busy means you are accomplishing something special.

- Productive people on the other hand know exactly what they want and they go for it. They use systems to track their progress and they work on the most important things first. They are selective with the use of their time and resources and figure out how to spend less time on getting the work done.

- Being productive means you are accomplishing tasks that will get you closer to meeting your goals. It means you have clear goals to work on. Running around like a headless chook without focus or a clear direction does not necessarily mean you are being productive!

Last but definitely not least, learn how to nip procrastination in the bud. Procrastination essentially wastes both your time and energy so it should be avoided at all costs.

40. HOW TO SET GOALS

Goal setting is another one of those skills that need to be specifically taught instead of just assuming everyone will master it on their own. You may or may not, but are you willing to take the risk?

So what's a goal? The term is defined as a clear, concise statement of what it is you wish to achieve. Setting goals is important as it usually gives your life direction and boosts your motivation and confidence. You will however need to:

a) Write these goals down and

b) Regularly focus on them, otherwise there is a good chance you may not achieve these goals.

In a nutshell, your goals should be SMART:

1. Specific

2. Measurable

3. Attainable

4. Relevant

5. Time-Bound

NOTE: It's not enough to say *I want to be healthy, wealthy, and happy*. These goals are too vague and undefined. What's wealthy? How much money do you want to have? How much do you want to make this year? The next five years? How are you going to do it?

Goal setting skills are essential so you will need to know how to establish a goal and how to take action towards it too, because a goal without a plan is just a wish. Action is imperative as explained by Greg S. Reid in the following quote:

"A dream written down with a date becomes a goal. A goal broken down into steps becomes a plan. A plan backed by action makes your dreams come true."

41. HOW TO DELEGATE

Delegating is when you entrust a task or responsibility to another person, typically one who is less senior than oneself. While it may seem that some kids are already experts in this field (delegating stuff to their parents!) this isn't quite what we had in mind when we decided to highlight this skill.

The reason why delegation is so important as an adult is because we can't feasibly DO EVERYTHING. Some of us may try but it only leads to lots of stress and heartache.

To delegate correctly here are some tips:

1. DELEGATE ONLY THINGS THAT ARE APPROPRIATE

This includes tasks that are not critical to you because you have higher priority tasks that demand your attention. Or delegate tasks that other people are more capable of doing or would benefit from learning. This includes tasks that have a lower cost to the value you can generate when doing other things. For example you may find a freelancer on Fiverr to do something cheaply when it would take you hours to achieve a lesser quality job.

DELEGATE TO THE RIGHT PEOPLE

You can't just pass a task to someone who has no intention of doing the job well. Make sure they have the time to carry out the requested job and that they have the knowledge and desire to do it too.

2. BE GRATEFUL

If someone is helping you out, shower them with praise for a job well done.

TIME TO BE
A GROWN-UP

42. HOW TO SAY "NO"

Adults who don't learn how to say "no" can end up with all sorts of issues. They are generally more stressed, over-committed, anxious, tired and often find themselves in situations they *are unable to get out of.

We all need to learn the art of saying no. You don't need to lie. You don't need to make excuses. You don't need to over-explain yourself or justify your actions. Refuse to please others at the expense of your emotional well-bring. Simply say the magic word NO and decline.

Remember when you say "yes" to others you need to make sure you are not saying "no" to yourself. Saying no to others isn't easy, but it's a required skill if you wish to have any degree of focus in your life. When you say no to others, understand that it is enough. NO is a complete sentence. It does not require justification or explanation. There is nothing wrong with saying no. Saying no means you know your limits. When you say no it gives you time to concentrate on things that are really important.

43. HOW TO BE A GOOD JUDGE OF CHARACTER

In life, our friends influence us more than we care to admit. This is why it is so important that you learn to assess whether someone is a good person, who will help you achieve your best, or a bad apple to steer clear of.

To become a good judge of character, consider the following tips:

- Consider how the person talks about other people. Do they generally speak highly of others or are they dismissive and gossipy behind their back?

- Look at what they are motivated by. Are they competitive or inclusive of others? What are their goals?

- Take note of their reliability. Can you depend on them to do what they say they will do? Do they keep their promises?

- Consider their actions: are they doing something that is typical of a person of good character or poor character?

- Look at how they treat people who are below them, how they act in pressure situations or react when in the wrong as these three circumstances can be highly revealing.

- Let go of your assumptions about people and understand that sometimes you are going to judge someone completely wrong. If it's the case, clean the slate and start again.

44. HOW TO ADMIT YOU WERE WRONG

Here's the thing. We all make mistakes. Mistakes are inevitable but they also have the power to turn you into something better than you were before. There is power in learning how to say, "I'm sorry, I was wrong," and taking responsibility for your mistakes. A person who can do that will be able to refocus, regroup and try again in work, in the classroom, in relationships and ultimately in life.

To be able to admit your faults takes effort, practice, and a change of attitude. This skill has the power to repair broken relationships, heal scars, and bring the conversation back to the important things in life.

Here are some tips to help master this skill:

- Know that the first to apologise is the bravest. The first to forgive is the strongest and the first to forget is the happiest.

- When you admit you are wrong, you are saying you are wiser now than you were before. You are ready and prepared to move on.

- Sometimes you need to swallow your pride and admit you were wrong. It's not called giving up; it's called growing up.

- It takes more courage to admit you made a mistake than to blame everyone else for your problems. Be brave and say sorry. No one in history has ever died from swallowing his or her pride.

- If you have to apologise, be humble about it. Say "I'm sorry your feelings were hurt." Mistakes are forgivable if one has the courage and strength to admit them.

- What hurts the most is when you don't admit you are wrong. It keeps you stuck in the same place, fuelled by anger, regret and weak. Be prepared to show some character and responsibility instead.

45. HOW TO BE TRUE TO YOURSELF

Here's the thing: you are a unique individual and one of a kind. It is especially vital that you understand the importance of maintaining your individuality once you are out in the real world. The world is going to try to make you conform, so you need to know it's okay to be different, okay to use your voice and okay to stand up tall and proud, even when you are alone.

To be true to yourself you need to understand the following:

- Know who you are, who you can potentially become, and how you can achieve this in life

- Understand your purpose and what brings you joy in your life

- Be prepared to live a fulfilling life and have a wide range of experiences in this world

- Understand each life stage has its own set of challenges, opportunities and obstacles

- Make excellent life choices that serve your best interests

- Learn how to stay focused on what is important and sensibly deal with distractions.

As Ralph Waldo Emerson said, "to be yourself in a world that is constantly trying to make you something else is the greatest accomplishment." We all want to fit in but where is joy and diversity in acting, looking, thinking the same as everyone else?

Humans were made to be different. We are all born looking different and grow up in different circumstances so in the end the most truly courageous act is to simply be YOU. Act and think for yourself and celebrate your individual differences because this will bring you true freedom.

46. HOW TO BE PATIENT

The key to patience is having the understanding that everything in this world takes time. Success or mastery of any skill is a process and it doesn't happen overnight. This is why it is so important to master this skill because patience is a gift. Everything is difficult before it becomes easy. Having patience will help you stay calm during the more stressful days.

To become more patient consider the following points:

- Note that patience is not the ability to wait but the ability to maintain a good attitude while you are waiting.

- Just because something isn't happening for you right now doesn't mean it will never happen.

- Even the nicest person's patience has a limit so learn to recognise yours. Be prepared to come up with some ideas of how you can cope when your patience is being sorely tested.

- If losing your patience is connected to losing your temper, stop letting people control so much of your mind, feelings and emotions.

- Every bad thing turns into a good thing in the end. It is all a matter of patience and waiting for the right moment.

- Finally remember the words of Mother Teresa: "Without patience, we will learn less in life, we will see less in life, we will feel less in life, we will hear less in life. Ironically *rush* and *more* usually mean less."

47. HOW TO KEEP GOING WHEN THE GOING GETS TOUGH

When the times get tough, it is important that you do not get discouraged or feel defeated.

Remember the following tips when faced with a challenge:

- Of course it's hard. It's supposed to be hard. If it were easy, everyone would be doing it.

- Don't give up just because you don't see results after a day or week. Even if you don't immediately see changes, every smart choice and decision you make is affecting you in ways you can't even imagine.

- Giving up is the easiest thing you could ever do, but holding it all together when everyone expects you to crumble is true strength.

- Brace yourself for the hurdles, and battles you are sure to face. Commitment means staying loyal to what you said you were going to do long after the mood has left you.

- As Socrates noted, the secret of change is to focus all of your energy not on fighting the old but on building the new. Do not be afraid to do this!

- Stay positive if you can and understand that these setbacks are just temporary. Everything is going to be okay in the end. If it's not okay, it's not the end.

48. HOW TO THINK FOR YOURSELF

At school, education is generally matter-of-fact which means students are tested on specific data or formulas they try to memorise, without giving too much thought to its process or how it can be applied in the real world.

Then at home we have parents who make decisions for their children without asking them first for their thoughts or feelings. This once again defeats the purpose of our ultimate goal, which is to raise children who know how to think for themselves!

So what exactly do we mean by the phrase "think for yourself"?

Mastery of this skill requires you to:

- Not be a robot or a puppet. You need to make decisions that are right for you instead of caving in to peer pressure

- Learn to critically question anything that goes against your better judgement. Question everything that doesn't sound right to you. Do not assume that someone else, even if they are in a position of authority, is always right.

- Use your own brain instead of depending on others for everything. If you can read, you can do research and learn to think for yourself.

- But be warned: thinking for yourself may cause a sudden outbreak of independence. It may also lead to wisdom, courage, confidence and power. A wise man makes his own decisions instead of ignorantly following public opinion.

- Remember the words of Albert Einstein: "The one who follows the crowd will usually get no further than the crowd. The one who walks alone, is likely to find himself in places no one has ever been."

- You were born an original so don't die a copy. A lion doesn't concern himself with the opinion of a sheep.

49. HOW TO RELAX

Knowing how to chill out and relax is important for your mental and physical health, particularly if your life is feeling stressful. Sometimes we feel like we don't deserve a break. Other times we don't give ourselves permission to sit down, when there are so many other tasks to attend to.

The ability to relax is however an important skill to master. You don't want to grow up to be a workaholic or stress-head, who is missing an easy "off" switch button. Relaxation is a skill you actually have to learn and practice, just like patience and happiness.

Remember you don't need to make every minute of the day "productive." You don't need to be attached to your phone or computer and respond to every message immediately. The time to relax is when you think you don't have time for it.

To relax and clear your mind, consider the following tips:

- When you are stressed, just stop, breathe in and breathe out – slowly, gently, deeply. Repeat this for a minute or until you feel calmer.

- Know there is as much virtue in rest as there is in work. Put up your feet when you need to. Lie down or lay your head on a cushion or pillow.

- Learn to meditate. And no, it isn't supposed to be complicated. Just find a comfortable spot in a quiet place, concentrate on your breath and let your mind drift away from all your anxieties and worries.

- Learn to take proper breaks frequently to avoid burnout. And not just little ones - proper breaks also include holidays, which we don't take often enough.

- Work out the best way to recharge your batteries: do you like to read or listen to music? Have a nap or go for a walk? Get a massage or go for a swim? Remind yourself to do these things often enough – or schedule them into your diary so you don't forget.

50. HOW TO MAKE A DECISION

Every day we are forced to make loads of decisions. As a kid, many of these choices are decided for us by the adults in our life, namely our parents. Then you get older and growing up suddenly means having to make your own grown-up decisions. But what if you haven't mastered this skill yet? What if you are constantly torn between being indecisive or simply uncertain? What if fear or a lack of confidence keeps you paralysed and standing in the same spot instead of moving forward?

Here are some tips on how to make an important decision:

- When making an important decision, ask yourself: does it take you closer to or farther away from your goals? If the answer is closer, take a leap of faith! If the answer is farther away, make a different choice. If you don't do it now, will you regret it?

- Another tip: when you need to make a hard decision, flip a coin. Why? Because when that coin is in the air you will suddenly know what it is you are hoping for. Alternatively list the pros and cons of each option. What does your heart tell you the right choice is?

- You will know that you made the right decision when you pick the hardest and most difficult option but your heart feels at peace.

- Sometimes in life you have to make decisions that are best for you but not for everyone else. Be confident with your choices and stop looking for other people's approval for everything. DO WHAT IS BEST FOR YOU! Everyone else is doing the same for themselves.

- Once you make a decision commit to it. Don't look back, instead make it work.

- If you insist on making silly or stupid decisions, don't be surprised when you see silly or stupid results.

- Allow your decisions to reflect your hopes NOT your fears! Whatever you decide to do, make sure it makes you happy. Sometimes it's the smallest decisions that can change your life forever.

- If you are indecisive remember this: a decision to do nothing is still a decision and may potentially be the worst one of all!

51. HOW TO PITCH IN

When everyone helps, everyone wins! These days parents seem to think that academics and activities are all that matter and they take care of everything else without realising this is actually hinders their children more than it helps them grow.

To run a household successfully, there are chores to be done and this cannot fall onto the shoulders of just one person. You will need to learn to contribute and pitch in for the betterment of the whole. You can't just expect others to serve you; you can't get away without ever doing something to help.

When it comes to your career, you may often need to do more than your expected tasks and you won't necessarily get a pat on the back for it either (applause will not be given to you as an adult for every great thing you do so don't expect it).

Tips on how to pitch in:

- Don't keep score. It isn't about who does or does not do more. Give freely of yourself and time without expecting anything in return.

- Be sincere with your help. There is no point in helping others if you have an ulterior motive. This just makes people feel indebted, uncomfortable and guilty. Pitch it because you want to help. Helping others achieve their dreams will help you achieve yours.

- The strongest people make time to help others, even if they are struggling with their own personal demons.

- Don't be more trouble than you are worth. If you are going to pitch in, be useful and don't intentionally cause other people stress or worry.

- Think about the words of St Mary of the Cross: "Never see a need without doing something about it." Find happiness in making others happy, stay calm and full of hope.

- Never underestimate the difference you can make in the lives of others. Reach out and offer your help when you can. People who come together and work as a community can make things happen. If we don't step up to help each other, who will? Be the good example that others can follow. Small acts, when multiplied by millions of people can transform the world. Expand your knowledge by expanding your community.

52. KNOW HOW TO DRESS WELL

First impressions are important therefore dressing well is an important skill to master. But what exactly does this mean? Tom Ford said "dressing well is a form of good manners" but I like to think it can be summed up in a few short grabs.

It means being tidy, dressing for your body shape, looking professional when required and staying up to date with fashion. Of course, fashion is what you buy and style is what you do with it, so it's a bonus if you can bring some of your personality into your outfit each day.

5 Tips on How to Dress To Impress

1. Have staple items in your closet that go with everything. For females, must-have items include a good pair of jeans, little black dress, black blazer, tailored pencil skirt and white shirt.

2. With work, understand what's appropriate in your industry. If your company has a dress-code, follow it!

3. Make sure your clothes fit you well. There is no point buying something that's too big or small for you. Dressing well means having clothes with a proper fit.

4. Accessorise well with the right accessories but don't overdo it. Accessories are meant to complement your outfit but not overpower it.

5. Finish it off with nice shoes and a good bag.

Keep in mind that clothes and style are a way of saying who you are to others without having to speak. It's okay to be different - in fact individuality in our clothing choices is both refreshing and special. Just don't look like you are trying too hard. You need to feel comfortable in the outfit you choose.

And remember, how you present yourself is how people view you and you will never get a second chance to make a great first impression. So what are you showcasing today?

53. HOW TO PACK YOUR BAG

Once upon a time, it was probably just a bad habit – having your parents pack your bag, even when you were at an age where you were capable of doing it yourself. But if you aren't careful that preschool backpack becomes a school bag and your school bag becomes a briefcase and before long you still haven't mastered the skill of being responsible for your own stuff.

You will need to learn how to do an inventory every morning of what you need for the day. Your list may include things like:

- Wallet

- Keys

- Cell phone

- Lunch

- Drink Bottle

- Books for school

- Laptop

Or when you reach an age where you can take an overnight trip yourself, you need to remember to pack the other essential items you can't leave home without, like:

- Toothbrush

- Toothpaste

- Hairbrush

- Razor

- PJs

- Underwear

- Socks

- Phone Charger

- Towel

- Deodorant

- Other toiletries

- Change of clothes

This list will vary according to where you are going and the length of time you will be away but the fact remains you need to be responsible for this task. If you are unsure of the sort of things you need to pack then google this information. You will find a plethora of lists for vacation, camping and other sorts of trips. Don't leave it up to someone else to do this job for you!

STUFF YOU JUST

NEED TO KNOW

54. KNOW HOW TO BE GRATEFUL

They say it's not happy people who are thankful; it's thankful people who are happy. Being grateful is that feeling of warmth or deep appreciation for something which has been done or received. It is a skill that some people need to be taught, especially if it doesn't come naturally to them. As William Arthur Ward noted, "gratitude can transform common days into thanksgiving, turn routine jobs into joy, and change ordinary opportunities into blessings."

To practice or master the skill of gratitude, consider the following tips:

- Start each day with a grateful heart. Count your blessings and not your problems. Make sure you don't compare yourself to others.

- Keep a gratitude journal. Write down at least five things you have to be grateful for each day. What are you grateful for today?

- Open your eyes to all the good things in your life. And yes, there is always something to be thankful for. Appreciate what you have right now.

- Understand that something good comes out of every bad situation. The happiest people do not have the best of everything. They make the best of everything.

- Tell others how much you appreciate them. Even better, write them a thank you note. Feeling gratitude and not expressing it like wrapping a present and not giving it – share it freely because gratitude is the best sort of gift.

- Ask yourself if you don't feel grateful with what you already have, what makes you think you will be happy with more? Happiness comes from the inside, not from the outside. If you concentrate only on what you don't have, you will never have enough.

- Learn to live in the moment. Enjoy each second as it passes, because it will never, ever come your way again.

- Control your thoughts. If you fall into a negative mood, you DO have the power to say STOP and to think of more positive things in your life. Don't get stuck focused on the past. It's time to let it go and move on. What's done is done. Focus on what you can do now to create a more beautiful future.

- Help others by volunteering your time, compassion or knowledge or giving what you can. There is nothing more rewarding than knowing you are positively impacting someone else's life.

55. KNOW YOUR VALUES

The following is an excerpt from my book "CREATE A LIFE YOU LOVE". It speaks about the importance of getting a clear idea of one's values because we all uphold certain values that dictate our preferred lifestyle, career and family life. When we're clear about our values, we tend to make our decisions proactively and with confidence.

A values assessment is therefore a critical step in discovering your passions, choosing an appropriate career and making choices in your life. Remember, it's difficult to be content with your life if you make decisions contrary to your values. Your values will provide you with a guide to living a content life.

STEP 1: Creating a list of your 20 most important values

Without giving thought to any order, peruse the list on the next page and tick off the 20 values that most speak out to you. Which of these values are fundamentally most important to you as a person? Which could you not live without in your life? This exercise is designed to give you a better understanding of your most significant values. So peruse the following list of values and note which ones are most important to you.

Abundance	Excitement	Intellectual status
Acceptance	Expertise	Intelligence
Advancement	Fairness	Kindness
Adventure	Family	Knowledge
Ambition	Fashion	Laughter
Animal Rights	Feminism	Leadership
Art	Financial Security	Learning
Authenticity	Flexibility	Leisure
Authority	Forgiveness	Literature
Balance	Frankness	Living my dreams
Beauty	Freedom of choice	Love
Calmness	Freedom w/ Time	Making a difference
Challenge	Friendships	Making decisions
Change	Fun	Morality
Charity	Generosity	Music
Clarity	Global Awareness	Nature
Collaboration	Happiness	Open communication
Color	Harmony	Optimism
Community	Having a voice	Organization
Compassion	Health	Passion
Competence	Helping Others	Patriotism
Competition	Helping Society	Peace
Courage	Honesty	Persistence
Creativity	Honor	Personal expression
Cultural diversity	Human Rights	Personal growth
Curiosity	Humor	Physical challenge
Decisiveness	Imagination	Play
Democracy	Independence	Pleasure
Discipline	Influence	Positive attitude
Empathy	Innovation	Power
Environment	Inspiration	Professionalism
Equality	Integrity	Quality of Life

Recognition

Reflection

Relationships

Relaxation

Reliability

Respect

Responsibility

Results

Risk taking

Security

Self-Love

Self-Respect

Sensuality

Spirituality

Spontaneity

Stability

Style

Support

Taking care of myself

Taking risks

The big picture

Tolerance

Tranquillity

Trust

Understanding

Variety

Wealth

STEP 2: Make a shortlist of your most important values

After you have perused the list, make a shortlist of your 20 most important values. Once you have done this you can then unearth your top five values by doing the following:

1.   Grouping together any similar values

2.   Removing values that are clearly not as significant as the others.

3.   Ultimately coming to a final decision by a process of elimination.

Your top five values are things that will make you feel more confident about making choices in your life. What did you decide was most important to you? Do you value respect and honesty? Is creative expression or personal growth important to you? Do you have a grounded sense of right and wrong? Do you know what you believe in and are you confident enough to live by these values?

It is not hard to make decisions once you know what your values are. When your values become clear to you, making decisions becomes easier. And this is important because sometimes it's the smallest decisions that change your life forever.

56. KNOW YOU ARE LOVED

One of the greatest gifts a person can venture off into the world with is the feeling that they are loved. You need to know that you are valued, cared for and have a purpose in life. You need to know that it doesn't matter if you don't look like everyone else or talk like everyone else or act like everyone else.

The simple fact is you are an individual and this is precious gift: there is no one else in the world like you. It's true that no one is perfect but hey, that's okay. You just need to do the best you can with what you have. You need to know you are a miracle.

As Pablo Casals so wisely said, "Since the beginning of the world there hasn't been, and until the end of the world there will not be, another child like him."

PARENT'S NOTE:

If you love your child share this information with him or her. It is the best feeling in the world to know someone loves you unconditionally. Feeling loved makes you feel safe and secure, valued and more optimistic. Out of all of the skills listed in this book, this one holds the most power and strength to create the greatest impact in your child's life.

57. KNOW SOMEONE

BELIEVES IN YOU

It is truly amazing how far we are willing to go when someone simply believes in us. Having this outside faith in our ability magically seems to push us to try harder, stay strong and never give up, even when we feel like throwing in the towel.

Now here's the good news – so many people actually DO believe in you. They know you can do it and they want you to succeed so let your faith be bigger than your fear. Of course, feeling scared sometimes is normal but when you start to doubt yourself remember everyone who believes in you. Sometimes all you need is someone to believe in you when it's too hard to believe in yourself.

We should point out though that millions of people can believe in you yet none of it matters **if you don't believe in yourself**. So say it out loud, even if it feels weird or strange at first: I BELIEVE IN MYSELF! Even if you feel you don't have the right support, that doesn't mean you should stop believing in yourself.

PARENT'S NOTE:

Just as it's important to tell your child how much you love them, it's important to share your belief in them too. Those four words "I believe in you" have the power to make the world of difference. If you feel these words are true, say it out loud to your child and say it often. Sometimes that is all they need to hear.

58. KNOW HOW TO DEAL
WITH PROBLEMS

In life there will always be problems: in fact one of our biggest problems is thinking we shouldn't have any problems!

To succeed in life, you are going to have to work out an effective way to deal with these hurdles, because yes, you will unfortunately face plenty along your journey.

Some tips on how to deal with problems effectively:

- Know you are either part of the problem or part of the solution – so which one do you want to be?

- When looking for a solution, stay focused on the problem, not the person, even if it is a person who created the problem in the first place. It's easier to keep emotions in check that way.

- Think with a clear head and rational mind. Stay calm and focused on the actual problem on hand, not other issues. To do this you will need to actually define the issue. And don't involve anyone that doesn't need to be involved.

- Remember a problem is only as big as you make it. All problems become smaller when you have the courage to face them, instead of running away or trying to dodge them.

Facing problems and working through them is what makes us strong.

- You need to talk things through with the person involved! Actively look for a solution or middle-ground compromise that you feel comfortable with. Be prepared to make some sacrifices too.

- When you focus too much on your problems, you will have more problems. When you focus on the possibilities, you will have more opportunities. Try to see the other person's perspective.

- When something bad happens you have three choices – you can either let it define you, let it destroy or let it strengthen you. Let go of things that you can't change.

- Sometimes the best solution to a problem is to open your heart and act with some maturity! Avoid any behaviour that makes the problem worse. Consider your options and choose the best plan for dealing with your current problem right now.

59. KNOW YOU ARE NOT THE CENTRE OF THE UNIVERSE

Mark Twain once said: *"Don't go around saying the world owes you a living. The world owes you nothing. It was here first."*

I first wrote about this tip in my book LIGHTBULB MOMENTS: 50 AHA! MOMENTS THAT WILL TRANSFORM YOUR LIFE. There I noted that this is one of scariest things about our current society - that the youth of today are growing up to be an entitled generation. When I was young, I expected nothing. If I wanted money or clothes or anything special, I knew I had to work for it. I was happy if someone was kind enough to throw me some craps. I appreciated every second-hand gift and didn't ever snarl at or question anything that was handed to me, advice included.

Nowadays kids seem to think everything should be handed to them on a silver platter. They think life owes them something – like a career, an adoring relationship, physical beauty, perfect health and comfort. They whinge and moan and complain when they don't get an award, a gift, a position or anything they want but don't have.

It's time to stop being a baby, develop a backbone and start behaving like a grownup. Be a responsible person. If you want something - whether it's happiness, wealth, power, success or love – you need to WORK for it yourself. You are NOT entitled to anything until you have saved and paid for it yourself.

You need to understand YOU ARE NOT THE CENTRE OF THE UNIVERSE! Life doesn't owe anyone anything: not perfect parents or a perfect childhood, not even immunity from pain or problems, a house, a bed, a job or even a single meal. If you haven't sweated or struggled for something, why do you think you deserve it?

Really, why? What makes you more special than previous generations who had to work hard for everything? Entitlement is an epidemic in this day and age and it is up to parents to model and teach our children the attitude of gratitude instead.

Note these facts:

- You can't always get what you want.

- You certainly don't deserve anything you didn't work for.

- You need to stop thinking like a victim.

- Take some personal responsibility instead of blaming life and other people for all the things you haven't achieved.

- We don't need to hear your stupid excuses. YOU don't need to hear your stupid excuses, even if you think they are valid and true.

All those "poor me" excuses hurt you more than they hurt anyone else because it equals DENIAL. Once you realise the truth – that you are NOT the centre of the universe and the world doesn't owe anyone anything – you can start to create your own happiness.

It is a GIFT when you acknowledge, accept and realise everything you DO have in your life needs to be earned. It is also a sign of maturity to know you are just one of many billions sharing this planet. So step up today and be prepared to stake your claim.

60. KNOW HOW TO RESPOND TO CRITICISM

Dealing with criticism is tough but it is a fact of life. Given that people will always have an opinion on what other people do , it's important to learn how to master this skill sooner rather than later. Criticism may not always be agreeable but it is a necessary part of life. If you are not open to constructive criticism then you are not truly open to growing as a person.

Here are some tips on how to accept criticism gracefully:

- Listen to everyone, no matter how painful it is. Whatever you do, good or bad, people will always have something negative to say. But don't automatically assume every critic is a hater because not everyone is trying to destroy you. Some people are telling you the truth.

- Acknowledge the good points made by the other party. You can disagree without being disrespectful. If it is untrue, disregard it. If it is unfair, don't allow it to irritate you. If it is ignorant, smile and ignore it. And if it is justified, learn from it.

- As Eleanor Roosevelt noted, "Do what you feel in your heart to be right – for you'll be criticized anyway. You'll be damned if you do, and damned if you don't."

Be open to criticism but don't be affected by it.

- People who say it cannot be done should not interrupt those who are actually doing it.

- Don't let people's compliments go to your head and don't let their criticism get to your heart. You can listen to criticism but learn how to take not it personally. Remember not everyone knows what's best for you because not everyone is YOU or living your life.

- Anyone who has done anything great has critics. Know the difference between your core values and when you are being stubborn. Criticism is meant to help you become a better person so learn from it.

- Consider that some criticism necessary for growth. Actively encourage others to give healthy critiques and learn to have thick skin. Don't take everything so personally!

- Ask yourself what can be learned from this criticism and don't hold a grudge. Was any part of the criticism useful? If so, learn from it. Otherwise let it go and stop letting people who do so little for you, control so much of your mind, feelings and emotions.

61. KNOW THE DIFFERENCE BETWEEN LOVE AND INFATUATION

When we're young, we fall in love furiously fast and it can seem like a rollercoaster ride of romantic stops and starts. We are also sometimes unable to differentiate the difference between lust or infatuation versus the long-term love that stable, loving relationships and marriages are built upon.

Here are some ways to help you differentiate the difference between healthy love and infatuation:

- Infatuation is when you find someone who is absolutely perfect. Love is when you realize they aren't perfect and it doesn't matter.

- Infatuation is when he ignores you but you like him anyway, when he does nothing yet you fall for him regardless, when you miss him even though he has never thought of you.

- Infatuation is blind while love is all-seeing and accepting. Love recognises the other person's fears and insecurities, flaws and blemishes and accepts them all.

- Infatuation is when you dream of everything that could be and wake up disappointed because it wasn't real. Love is when you have nightmares of losing what you have, and you wake up relieved that it was only a dream.

- Infatuation is a short-lived passion for someone whereas love is a deep affection that lasts the test of time. Only problem is that infatuation is such an intense feeling that it makes you feel as if you are in love.

- Infatuation is the state of being completely lost in the emotion of unreasoning desire. Love is the willingness to make sacrifices for each other and working hard to settle differences.

- Infatuation is the crazy, reckless feeling to satisfy your lust while love is the genuine commitment to each other, with genuine, heartfelt intentions. In the latter form, you are confident, content, patient, secure and peaceful instead of feeling empty or lost.

- Infatuation cannot be sustained forever without some portion of love. it is fast and furious and can leave you feeling empty whereas real love deepens with the passage of time.

- Don't mistake a temporary infatuation with real love as you could end up with long-term regrets. Go with your gut feeling. Does your relationship feel healthy or one-sided? Does it make you feel happy or sad inside? Sometimes the questions are that simple.

62. KNOW YOUR PARENTS ARE PEOPLE TOO

It's weird to think that once upon a time your parents were young too. As I explained in my book INSPIRING TEENS: HOW TO LIVE LIFE WITHOUT REGRET, your parents are ordinary, fallible people just like you. Once upon a time, they had their first kiss, first love, first heartbreak, first rejection, first job, first everything in life just like you have had or are about to have. Even though it doesn't seem like it, parents can be a wealth of wisdom and experience.

But they aren't perfect, aren't they? Because there is no such thing as a perfect parent just as there is no such thing as a perfect child. They are going to sometimes (or often) say stupid things. They are going to give you bad advice or seem like they haven't the faintest idea what you are going through.

Nonetheless most parents want the best for their child. They will do what they think is right for you, given the skills they have, even if these skills fall short of both your and their expectations. They are human too, which means they will have their good and bad days. They will have their own battles and problems to worry about.

Being an adult means they have additional responsibilities that a teenager doesn't have to think or stress about, like bills and a mortgage that needs to be paid, meals to be organized, a house to clean and children to raise. Sometimes when we are so busy growing up we forget our parents are also growing old and they have their own dreams to chase and fulfil.

Even though they may not be perfect, even if you think they are annoying or old-fashioned, crazy or too strict, try to appreciate your parents. Never complain about what your parents couldn't give up – it was probably all they had. You will never know what sacrifices they went through for you.

Ask them questions as questions lead to understanding. Respect and honor them as they do want the best for you, even if it feels more like it's the best for them. Finally love your parents and treat them with care, for you will only know their value when you see their empty chair.

63. KNOW WHERE TO TURN
FOR HELP

When you are young, help is usually always there in the form of your parents but one day Mom and Dad might not always be there. It is up to you to learn the skill of knowing where to turn for help elsewhere. Are you confident in finding or building a community of support? What kind of support system do you already have in place other than home?

Some options for people and organizations that are usually willing to help when required:

- Friends and other family members

- Other adults you can trust

- Teachers and staff at schools and colleges

- Local church leaders and members

- Your local GP and hospitals

- Psychologists

- Community health services

- Various support groups within your state – search for this information online if your local community centre is unable to provide it

- Online support groups where you can sometimes request help anonymously

- Rehabilitation and support programs

- Career support agencies

- Respite and financial assistance

Many of us don't like to ask for help as we feel uncomfortable, as if it is a sign of weakness. Do not assume that people are mind-readers – if you are in trouble or need help, it is okay to share your thoughts and feeling with others.

It is okay to ask for help! People are more willing to help than you might assume. We all have two hands – one to help ourselves, the second to help others. Even if we can't help everyone, everyone can help someone and there will be someone out there who can and will help lighten your load. The only mistake you can make is not asking for help when you need it.

64. KNOW WHAT YOU ARE GOOD AT

Confucius once wisely said: "Choose a job you love and you will never have to work a day in your life." Now while success means different things to different people, there is a better chance you will create your own personal success story if you know what you are good at and what you want to be better at.

Think about all the things you love to do – whether it is writing, acting, helping or entertaining others, designing or building things. Your interests will give you a clue as to what you might enjoy doing in your work or career, once you finish school. It is so much easier going to work when you love what you do.

Thankfully we have all been given special gifts and strengths. Even if you don't know what it is just yet, that doesn't mean it isn't there or that you don't have one. We all are good at something! When the time comes that you suddenly realise you are really great at something don't be afraid to use your gift. You were given it for a reason.

This means EVERYONE has something special to offer so don't be scared to make your own personal contribution just because you think someone else is better at it than you.

Every single person in this world has a gift of some kind and this includes things like kindness, creativity and courage. Or it could be other attributes like patience, decisiveness, responsibility, organisation, enthusiasm, and persuasion.

You need to work out what your strengths are so you can use them. If you truly have no idea, ask your family and friends what they think your skills may be as they would have surely noticed the things you are good at. Knowing your strengths creates self-confidence, increases your sense of accomplishment, and opens doors that otherwise would have been closed. Be proud of what you can do and share it with the world.

NOTHING WRONG WITH BEING

A SMARTY-PANTS

65. HOW TO PREPARE AND WRITE A RESUME

Every young adult should know how to write out an impressive resume that lists all their strengths, skills, and accomplishments. This can be practiced in your teen years so that by the time you are ready to find a real job, writing a resume won't feel so difficult and you will know exactly what to write to impress future employees.

To write a great resume consider the following tips:

- Take the time to work out what to include on your resume. What are your most important skills and experience?

- Do your research. Your resume is a marketing tool that needs to demonstrate that you have the right qualifications and skills for the job. Search different templates online to see how you can convey this information in a professional way.

- There is usually no set length for a resume, as its length will vary depending on your experience. One or two pages is perfect, if you can succinctly include all relevant information in this space. DO NOT fill it with unnecessary information just to make it longer.

- There is usually a specific order which needs to be followed when writing a resume. It is as follows:

  - Contact details
  - Opening statements
  - List of key skills and personal attributes
  - Educational qualifications
  - Employment history include work experience
  - References and referees

- You may need to tailor your resume for each different job application, so that you can highlight your skills and strengths for the specific requirements they have.

- Note that you aren't obliged to include private information on your resume like your birthdate, gender, address, disabilities or health status. Only do so if you think this works in your favour.

- Finally remember that your resume is an opportunity to make a first impression. It is an important marketing tool so make sure it has no spelling errors, you aren't making any demands and that it does not include any irrelevant or damaging information.

- NOTE: If you have no work experience that's okay too. You can instead emphasise your education and all the transferable skills you may have gained during extracurricular activities, internships or volunteering.

66. HOW TO STUDY

You would hope that by the time you reach high school you will have worked out the secret to successful studying but the truth is studying is an art that is seldom taught to students. Many kids make it to college without knowing the proper technique to study. Newsflash: it is not enough to simply read a textbook a few times!

To study properly you will need to:

- Identify what you are expected to know. What are the main points of the lesson? Highlight any important details.

- Summarise your work or outline the material as it is easier when the main ideas have been organised in point form.

- Know how to practice testing yourself before the real test. You won't necessarily be hand fed your test information or answers so you will need to learn how to think outside the square.

- Break down big things into smaller sections. Make flash cards with the most important information written down. Rewriting your notes helps you to learn.

- If possible make associations with the material you need to memorise as this is the most effective way to retain information.

- Manage your time well. You will need to stick to your schedule as much as possible with a lot of time given for preparation and revision.

- Get enough sleep – this will need to be factored into your schedule. Eat well too as you study better when you take care of yourself.

- Set up a good study space where you are comfortable and it is relatively quiet.

- Take breaks often and eliminate distractions.

- Join a study group if this works for you as you can quiz each other.

- Work out your preferred way of learning. Some of us are auditory learners (who learn by listening), others are visual learners (who learn by seeing) and others are tactile learners (who learn by doing).

- Stay motivated – it helps if you remind yourself often of your ultimate goals.

67. HOW TO PROOFREAD

Proofreading means examining your text carefully to find and correct any typographical errors and mistakes in grammar, style and spelling. While little errors may be overlooked when your child is in high school, the fact remains that college professors or work colleagues won't look so kindly over silly mistakes.

Here are some tips to proofread well:

- Give it a rest. If time allows for this, set aside your text for a few hours or days after you have finished composing it and then proofread it with fresh eyes.

- Double-check any facts, figures or spelling of names.

- Always review a printed version of your work – this may help you catch some errors that you previously missed.

- Use a spellcheck if you aren't sure about the spelling of difficult words.

- Read your text aloud to catch any grammatical errors

- Ask someone else to proofread your text as they may immediately spot an error you have missed.

68. HOW TO USE A DICTIONARY

For the older generation, many would have owned a hardback dictionary back in middle school and been encouraged to look up new words or double check meanings of words they weren't so sure about. This seems to be a lost art with the advent of computers and automatic spell-check, which is such a shame.

There is no reason why we can't keep on expanding our vocabulary as adults. Referring to a dictionary also reinforces learning alphabetical order and is great for retention as well.

Here are some tips on how to use a dictionary:

- Have one on hand on your bookshelf. It is hard to use what you cannot see!

- Learn the abbreviations that are used in dictionaries. For example, ADJ usually stands for adjective, ADVB for adverb, N for noun and V for verb.

- Understand the guide to pronunciation. A dictionary often has symbols that will help make pronunciation easier for you. If you are still unsure you can google your difficult word alongside the term pronunciation and there's a good chance it will play the correct pronunciation out loud for you.

- A thesaurus is another fantastic resource which will give you the synonym (word that means nearly the same) or antonym (word that means nearly the opposite) of most common terms.

- Commit to learning a new word every day. You can expand your vocabulary immensely if you look up any new words you hear or read but don't know the meaning to. Or you can randomly read entries of words you aren't yet familiar with.

69. HOW TO IDENTIFY A POTENTIAL SCAM

Scams are any scheme that exists to try and con you out of money. It can arrive by post, phone call, text message or email (or sometimes even show up in person on your front doorstep!) It would be great to think you would never fall for a scam but the truth is you will need to be taught how to identify a potential scam, as all age groups can be targeted by scammers.

Some simple tips to keep in mind regarding scams:

- If it sounds easy or too good to be true; it probably is.

- If you have to forward something or re-post it, it is probably also a scam.

- Do not ever share personal financial information or passwords to anyone who solicits a charitable donation from you.

- Know that scammers are the masters of emotional manipulation. They want you to feel scared about getting into trouble or excited about a potential windfall. DO NOT believe anyone who calls you and demands to receive private information off you via the telephone or via the internet.

- Why is it so important to keep your private information private? Because this information can be used to access your bank accounts, take out loans in your name and lodge false tax returns.

- If you get a call, ask the caller for their full name and extension number and their team leader's full name and extension number so you can later verify the call.

- It is always best to be wary. Better to be safe than sorry!

70. HOW TO SEND A PROFESSIONAL EMAIL

Knowing how to write a professional email is a must nowadays because so much information happens via this method. You will need to know how to convey your message in a clear and respectful way, even when you are not speaking face to face with people.

To write a professional email, consider the following advice:

- Always fill the subject line with a topic that means something to your reader.

- Begin with a polite greeting such as "Dear so-and-so" or "To Whom It May Concern"

- Thank the recipient for taking the time to read your email.

- Simply state your purpose. Put your main point in the first sentence. Clear emails always have a clear purpose.

- If you are introducing yourself for the first time, please keep the introduction brief.

- Add your closing remarks such as "thank you for your help with this", "I look forward to hearing your response" or "Should you have any further questions please do not hesitate to contact me."

- End with a closing such as "Wishing you warm regards" or "Yours sincerely".

- DO NOT write in all capitals as this will come across as if you are shouting.

- Please do not use any emojis or funny abbreviations like LOL.

- Be brief and polite and remember to say "please" and "thank you".

- Add a signature block with appropriate contact information. This will usually include your full name, business address and phone number.

- Edit and proofread your email before hitting "send."

- Reply promptly to important emails. If you think you need more than 24 hours to properly response, add a brief response explaining your delay.

71. HOW TO WRITE AN ESSAY

Essays are an essential part of homework when you are a student in high school and college and they will often be found as part of your tests. The purpose of a good essay is to persuade readers of an idea based on evidence. Mastering this skill is important if you want to do well in school, and later in life too if you are in a position where you must persuade others using your words.

Consider the following tips on how to write a great essay:

- Essays generally follow a specific format. They should answer a specific question or task, have an argument and should include relevant examples, supporting evidence and information from credible sources.

- To write an essay, analyse the question and define the key terms in the question. Use a dictionary to check the meaning of any unfamiliar words.

- Research the topic widely, using books, journals and credible academic sources for supporting evidence.

- Brainstorm and establish the point of view you may wish to take.

- Take notes from your research and order your ideas in a logical sequence.

- Come up with a plan and begin to organise your ideas. Make sure every point is relevant to the essay question.

- Draft an introduction and body to your essay. Each point is to be written in a new paragraph. Provide supporting evidence for each point you make.

- Come back later to edit your work and make any appropriate changes.

- In your conclusion, summarise your main ideas, demonstrate how you have proven your thesis and finish with an interesting or thought-provoking but relevant statement.

- Write out your references and citations.

- Complete your final draft and present a clean, note copy before the deadline.

72. HOW TO KEEP YOUR COMPUTER SECURE

Nowadays it is absolutely critical that we learn to keep our computers secure. Because we store so much important data on our computers, we need to make sure our computers stay secure and our personal data remains as private as possible.

Here are some basic tips to keeping your computer safe on the internet:

1. Get a firewall.

A firewall is a barrier between something you want to keep safe and something that is potentially dangerous. This software or hardware sits between your computer and internet and only allows certain types of data to cross.

2. Scan for malware.

Malware is short for malicious software and it is most commonly received via email attachments. A malware scanner locates and removes the virus from your hard drive. Because new malware is being created every day it is absolutely essential that you keep your anti-malware software up-to-date. Be sure to enable the scanning to take place every day.

3. Enable automatic updates

The solution to keeping infections at bay is to enable automatic updates on your computer and applications.

4. Be knowledgeable and conscious of the possibilities of threats

It is up to YOU to make sure you don't expose yourself to threats. You can do this by not opening attachments unless you are positive they are fine, don't click on any links in emails unless you are positive they are safe and don't install "free" software without checking it out first. These often come loaded with spyware, adware and other bad stuff so you really need to be vigilant about avoiding them.

Also never, ever click on any pop-up ad – even if it says your computer is infected or has a problem! It is just a ruse! Avoid using peer-to-peer software for copyrighted movies and software as there is a good chance they will contain a virus. Choose secure passwords too and never share divulge sensitive information with anyone, or you run the risk of exposing your computer to unwanted threats.

Finally secure your Wi-Fi at home and be careful when using free Wi-Fi or personal hotspots as this opens you up to people stealing your personal information if the connection isn't encrypted and secure.

73. HOW TO BACK UP YOUR DATA

Once upon a time if a person was asked to name what he or she would save in a fire the top item on most lists would be photo albums. We all know that nowadays the majority of our precious pics are stored on a computer and hard drive.

These days our most important data is stored on our computer – this included photos, important emails and documents, music, research papers and more. Losing this stuff is what nightmares are made of so we need to do whatever we can to save it.

Creating a backup before anything goes wrong is an important skill to master as a new-age, responsible computer user. Thankfully it isn't a difficult task and the steps to accomplish this are simple:

- Purchase an external hard-drive or USB which is to be purely used for storing backups. Make sure you backup these files regularly – at the very least, once a week.

- Hardware can break so it's important to have an extra copy of all your most important data. Purchase an additional backup drive or USB and keep it stored in a safe place (like your parent's place). This extra backup can be updated less regularly but ideally once a month would perfect.

- Consider having a cloud backup as these are the easiest to create and maintain. Examples include: Dropbox, OneDrive and Google Drive - these services make it incredibly easy to make free backups of your files.

You can also pay a reasonable monthly or yearly fee to get a lot more storage.

- You should also regularly run a full Windows PC or laptop backup. Good backup software should schedule backups so they take place automatically at regular intervals.

74. HOW TO READ OFFICIAL DOCUMENTS

Even if you are not a keen reader of books, the fact remains that you will still need to read and process written material in your adult life, especially if you want to master the skill of understanding official documents.

Why is it so important to understand official documents? Because they are the bane of our adult existence – even our most favourite activities like driving and travelling all require important documents to be filled out beforehand. As an adult you will need to file your own taxes, apply for a passport, get a driver's licence, purchase a property or sign a rental agreement.

All of these require official documents to be filled in and signed and it isn't something you can expect your mom and dad to do forever.

Some basic tips on how to process an official document:

- First and foremost read the whole thing. Make sure you understand the purpose of the document and the most important points covered. Who is it from? What is its purpose? When is it due back by? Where does it need to be returned?

- Don't be intimidated. Seek help if you need it. Many legal terms can be found explained on the internet. For example: *herein= in or inside here, shall = must, forthwith= at once or immediately.* When all else fails, contact a lawyer.

- Write neatly. You need to be legible, otherwise you risk having to fill the form in again.

- If you have to return the form with additional documentation, make sure to make a copy of everything before you send it in case it gets lost.

75. HOW TO SEARCH
GOOGLE LIKE A PRO

Once upon a time, we had to go to the library or ask a hopefully wise grownup if we wanted the answer to something. Now we can find the answer to even the craziest questions within seconds using the Internet. Google is an incredible tool yet not everyone knows how to utilise it properly.

Here are some tips on how to search Google like a pro:

- Don't just ask Google questions. Think about other ways that an answer might be phrased and search for that instead.

- Google will define any word for you if you write **define:** in front of any word you want.

- For quick basic mathematical problems, simply type the equation into Google and it will give you the answer

- You can also use Google to do unit conversions. For example, 10 miles in KM or 60 KG in pounds.

- Use Google like a stop watch by *entering set timer for* followed by the amount of time you need.

- Or you can compare foods using **"vs"** and you will receive comparisons of nutritional facts.

- Google will also translate words or phrases into different languages too if you ask it to.

- Finally Google provides the easiest and quickest way to perform a plagiarism check to see if a work has been plagiarised. You can also use Google Scholar software to scan your research paper and essay to make sure it isn't plagiarised.

Here's an overview of the most useful Google search tricks:

Site:

If you write site: in front of a page, Google will only search the pages of that site. For example: site: dailymirror.co.uk

" "

Inverted commons around a word or phrase means Google will search for the exact phrase, no each of the words separately.

-

A minus sign before a word will excludes this term from the search.

~

Google will also search related words if this symbol is placed before a word

..

Two full stops between a date range means Google will only shows all results from within the designated date range. For example: 1975..2000

Filetype:

Google will only searches results of the file type you are after if you specify what you are after. For example, filetype:pdf, filetype:doc or filetype:jpg.

Intitle:

If you include this before a word Google will only shows results with that word in the title. For example, intitle:happiness.

*

When you include this asterisk symbol before a word Google will replace it with common terms in your search. For example, * is thicker than water.

As a final note, I should point out that if you need any extra information on the skills provided in this book, including how-to videos, Google is the first place I recommend you visit. There you can find just about anything you're looking for.

76. HOW TO DETECT A LIE

Learning how to detect when someone is lying to you may seem like a weird skill to master but the truth is this can be especially useful when dealing with work colleagues, strangers or suspicious friends and family members.

According to research, most humans lie on a regular basis and over half of adults can't have a 10 minute conversation without lying at least once. Now obviously there is a difference between the little white lies and the big, bad ones, but even still, a lie is still a lie. Here are some tips to help you work out when someone is telling you a porky.

NON VERBAL SIGNALS TO DETECT A LIE

- **EYES:**

  Blinking rate will increase from the normal 10 blinks per minute, up to 60 blinks per minute when someone is lying. Denying eye contact is also a sign, so look out for eyes that are constantly wavering, especially during a touchy subject.

- **SLOWER SPEECH or HESITATION:**

  A liar will usually make up events while speaking and hesitate while thinking of a lie to fit into the occasion.

- **CHANGE OF TONE**

  Listen for higher or lower pitch tones than a person's normal speech as this change is common when lying.

- **BODY POSTURE:**

  Do they constantly shift their stance? Do they pull their body inward, become squirmy or conceal their hands to subconsciously hide their fidgety fingers? More signs of lying.

- **FACE:**

  Look for micro-expressions such as eyebrows being drawn upwards. People also tend to touch their nose more when lying.

OTHER THINGS TO BE SUSPCIOUS OF:

- Do they instantly change the topic? Do they have exaggerated movements? Do they deflect questions or repeat their sentences?

- Do they react well to your questions? Do their answers seem impulsive or delayed? Do their sentences jump? Do they repeat their words? Are they providing too much information?

- Are they sweaty or blushing? Do they gulp or clear their throat often? Do they play with their hair or adjust their tie? Do they fold their arms as if they are being defensive? Use these signals to work out what's a lie and what's the truth.

77. HOW TO PLAN AN EVENT

When you're young, everything is usually planned out for you but as you grow older this responsibility falls on your own shoulders. As soon as you are old enough, it is expected that you will organise the details of an event yourself. For example, if you are going to the moves you will need to arrange the drop-off time, meeting point, purchase of the tickets, money for the outing and what time it will end.

Event planning is important for every activity under the sun. Things like date, time and an itinerary should be planned well in advance to the event.

To plan a successful event you will need to organise the following things:

- Choose the right venue

- Set a goal for the event – what are you planning to do or achieve?

- Identify what you need for this event

- Work out a budget for each person

- Organise transport

- Decide who is invited to the event and an RSVP date by which you need attendance confirmed

- Have a plan B in case your initial plan doesn't work out, due to weather or other conditions

- Enjoy yourself and afterwards thank those who attended.

78. HOW TO MANAGE

SOCIAL MEDIA

In many ways social media is a great thing – people use it to interact with others, form communities and build connections with people who share common goals and interests. In theory it seems fantastic – we feel as sense of connection and belonging to our family, friends and peers when we use this form of communication.

Then there is the downside. The more time we spend on the internet the more we expose ourselves to people who can humiliate, bully or stalk us. There is even the potential to connect with someone who wants to harm us. And suddenly what seemed like a great thing is not so great after all...

Because social media is the new norm, it is crucial that you learn to manage social media well, lest it ruins your life. Does that sound rather dramatic? Well think again, for many teens and young adults have made mistakes on social media they regret and that still live to haunt their lives years later.

You absolutely need to learn how to stay safe when it comes to sharing information freely with the world.

Here are some tips on how to manage social media, (rather than allowing it to rule your life):

- ## DON'T ALLOW IT TO BECOME AN OBSESSION

It is honestly easy to waste hours each day on social media – WAY TOO EASY. For some people it becomes more than just an occasional hobby. Instead it becomes an "addiction" and they can't help but spend hours staring at their phones. Consider taking a break from social media or limiting the time you spend online. One hour a day is more than enough to see and do what needs to be seen and done (probably too much). If you are used to spending more than this, consider delaying your use until after you have completed your more important and urgent tasks.

- ## PROTECT YOUR PRIVACY

You will need to work out your own way to stay safe and protect your reputation while enjoying social media in your life. See it for what it is: a simple tool – a tool you need to stay control of instead of allowing it to control you. Don't share your private information with the world. Set your profile to private. Don't assume that your friends will always be your friends so remember anything you share can be used against you in the future.

- ## DON'T MISTAKE IT FOR REAL CONNECTIONS

Even though you think you are "connecting" with others when you use social media, real connection takes place face-to-face or when you pick up the phone. Your life on the internet is NOT your real life. Social skills are crucial in the workplace but you rob yourself of the opportunity to build them when you spend more time staring at a screen rather than into the eyes of a fellow human being.

- ## DON'T DEFINE YOURSELF BY WHAT OTHER PEOPLE SAY ABOUT YOU

Try not to be so desperate that you crave positive feedback from strangers or people you don't know or care for.

- ## UNDERSTAND THAT SOCIAL MEDIA IS THE NEW PERMANENT RECORD

What you post never goes away – it will stay there in the land of abyss forever. Today photos and posts are more like tattoos. What you post online will be there forever; even when you die, it lives on forever. It doesn't matter if you change your mind two minutes after posting something and take it down. Technology has evolved to the point where people can screenshot a picture or record the evidence using a different device to make a record of your transgression.

- ## UNDERSTAND PEOPLE ALWAYS PUT THEIR BEST FOOT FORWARD ON THE INTERNET

Their posts only provide a tiny snapshot of their life. People post their best pics (after culling them from a hundred bad ones and filtering them to perfection) and these photos paint a rosy picture which never tells anyone the whole true story. Be less concerned with how your life looks to others and more concerned with how you feel about yourself.

- ## THINK TWICE BEFORE YOU POST ANYTHING

Once upon a time you could say something negative about someone and it would be forgotten over time or you could deny (if you needed to) that it ever happened. Nowadays however, nope we are not nearly as lucky anymore. So think twice before you post anything. Something you think is funny today can be humiliating or stupid the next day. Something you write out of anger or sadness can come back to bite you in the butt.

- ## UNDERSTAND THINGS CAN BE TAKEN OUT OF CONTEXT

Words, photos and videos of you can be taken out of context and twisted to mean something else so guard your privacy and reputation like it's the most precious thing in the world. Because guess what – it is!

Comments, actions or images you post online can stay online long after you decide to delete the material. You will never truly know who else has seen it. None of us can comprehend the true power of the internet that allows strangers, even creepy people you want to avoid, to tap into your most personal moments and memories. So think carefully about what you choose to document.

KNOW YOUR RIGHTS

So what do you do if someone is bullying you online or has posted something negative about you? Firstly it helps to understand your rights. Cyberbullying is bullying that is done through the use of technology. It is important to know each state and country has different laws for bullying and you should seek legal advice if you wish to prosecute the offender. Everyone has the right to be respected, safe, and free from violence, harassment and bullying.

A life free from cruel, degrading or inhumane treatment is one of our fundamental human rights. If this happens to you make sure you keep the evidence and screenshot a record of what you have seen. Don't feel defeated if the post is anonymous – detectives are equipped to trace IP addresses and will usually be able to track down the culprit. If you have seen something on Facebook you can flag and report the incident to their staff and they will take it down for you.

79. MASTER BASIC MATH

It is honestly surprisingly how few people finish school without being able to complete basic math efficiently or at all. You cannot assume you will be able to depend on a calculator in life! Mathematics is important in life because it is used to perform so many different basic daily tasks, such as telling the time, counting change and reading an odometer. It is even more so important when considering interest rates, investment options and considering the probability of things.

While there's not nearly enough space here to cover the fundamentals of basic math, here are the concepts you should be familiar with by the time you reach adulthood:

- Addition and Subtraction (1-100 – you should be quick as sticks with this!)

- Multiplication times-table (for 1-12 – you must also be able to do this proficiently!)

- Understand decimals and fractions

- Know how to calculate percentages

- Know how to convert between fractions, decimals and percentages

- Know how to work out a unit price (per litre or kilo) so that you know what the best deal is

Maybe these skills don't seem important to you right now or you don't understand yet how they can be applied in the real world but trust me when I say that you will use this skill more than you would have ever expected to. Knowing math will increase your ability to perform at your job and in life.

If you aren't proficient with these basic skills, it is never too late to learn and practice it. Keep practicing until it becomes second nature and it is something you can do "inside your head." Mastering basic arithmetic will allow you to make better decisions and help you to better understand the world.

80. VALUE LEARNING

You may have read this heading and thought "Ah, seriously? Haven't I had enough of this learning stuff, given that I've been in school since around age five?" Well I'm afraid to break the news to you but learning isn't something you just give up doing the day you graduate from high school or college.

Albert Einstein once said, "Once you stop learning, you start dying." This sounds like a rather harsh statement but the fact remains that all of life is a learning experience. The more you open your eyes and embrace life's lessons, and the more you are WILLING to learn, then the more you get out of life.

Some tips on the importance of learning:

- Understand that what we learn becomes a part of who we are. Learning isn't just about the boring stuff, teachers and textbooks. It's about being open to learning from your mistakes, from positive role models, from your family and friends.

- Learning is also not something that is done to you. It is something you choose to do. You are responsible for that choice. Do you want to learn and grow or remain stubborn and stagnant? It is all up to you.

- Never stop learning because life never stops teaching. If you are not willing to learn, no one can help you. If you are determined to learn, no one can stop you. What you learn can never be taken away from you.

- To truly grow, you need to push yourself beyond what you already know and have mastered. You need to step outside your comfort zone, admit you don't know and search for answers.

- Commit yourself to a life full of learning. You are never, ever too old to learn something new.

- Finally note the wise words of Henry Ford, "Anyone who stops learning is old, whether at twenty or eighty. Anyone who keeps learning stays young. The greatest thing in life is to keep your mind young."

81. VALUE THINGS BESIDE MATERIAL POSSESSIONS

As kids we are often taught to save for the special, big-ticket items assuming that they will bring us happiness. Then we learn, often the hard way that the little hole inside our heart cannot be filled by material possessions. Some of us don't discover this until a lot later in life, after they have already accumulated the big house, fancy car and all the latest pieces of technology on offer.

As discussed in my book LIGHTBULB MOMENTS: 50 AHA! MOMENTS THAT WILL TRANSFORM YOUR LIFE, some of the most precious things in this world are things you cannot buy and do not have a price tag attached to them. These things are not only free but priceless.

These precious gifts are the people you love, the places you have seen and the memories you have made along the way. They include: hugs, kisses, smiles, friends, family, sleep, love, laughter, music, good advice, great books, fresh air and good memories.

You will need to learn how to value things besides material possessions. That's because the best things in life are not something you can touch but something that you can feel. It is important never to lose sight of this. Life is priceless, family is a treasure, friends are a blessing, time is gold and health is wealth. In a nutshell, the best things in life are free.

BE AN ALL-ROUND GRACIOUS, KIND HUMAN BEING

82. HOW TO DEFUSE
POTENTIAL CONFLICT

Many of us have a natural tendency to defend ourselves when confronted. There are times when meeting strength with strength is appropriate, but there are also moments when we need to know how to gracefully back out of a developing conflict, before it leads to a dangerous escalation. It is important to know when a situation calls for a peacemaker, and how to be that person.

Here are some important tips on how to defuse potential conflict when the situation calls for it:

- Watch out for the warning signs that conflict is brewing. Try to remain calm and see the other person's point of view.

- Listen to and clarify exactly what the problem is. Why is the other person so angry or upset? Try to understand what they are going through. What pressure may they be under and what is it they are trying to achieve?

- Be emphatic and understanding. You need to appreciate and acknowledge their different opinions and be open to making a small concession if required.

- Apologise if you have to. You can say "I'm sorry you are so upset" or "Let's try to work out a solution to moving forward."

- Find some common ground that you can work towards. React positively to any constructive feedback, take responsibility for your own actions and decide what you can agree upon. Remember there are two sides to every story.

- Take emotion out of the equation. Focus instead on the facts, priorities and task at hand. You can be calm and assertive without being aggressive.

- Work out a solution that you can both agree on. Keep communication open without getting too stressed or anxious about the conflict.

- Conflict is normal and shouldn't be feared. Instead it needs to be properly managed. It is most effectively resolved using dialogue, as humans are just trying to understand each other.

- Remember conflict cannot continue without your participation. Learn to let some things go as happiness is not found in conflict but in peace and making resolutions you feel comfortable with.

83. HOW TO ADVOCATE FOR YOURSELF

Being an advocate means learning to speak up and use your voice, defending yourself when necessary and also understanding you have the right to fight for your rights and support when you need it. Here's the deal - your mum and dad cannot advocate for you forever. One day you are going to have to learn to stand up for yourself. If you aren't happy with something, you need to be capable of doing this yourself, instead of assuming you can just send someone else in to help or save the day. The truth is you can do it.

Here are some important tips to remember along the way:

- You have the right to ensure you have the same chances in life, same rights and same choices in life as everyone else. KNOW THIS!

- You need to make sure you are actively involved in the decisions that affect you. SO BE INVOLVED IN THIS!

- It's okay to ask for help when you need it. Be willing to ask questions and understand that sometimes you won't get the outcome you desire. The important thing is that you are generally in charge of your own life.

- Believe in yourself and know your rights. Decide what you want and get the facts. Express yourself clearly and assert yourself calmly. Be firm and persistent when necessary.

84. HOW TO WRITE A THANK YOU LETTER

For way too long, people have struggled with the right way to say thank you. We sometimes think we don't need to say it out loud (as if the person just somehow knows!) or we send our message in a quick text or email as if that will suffice. And maybe that does do the job on occasions but you should also know there is nothing quite as fabulous as receiving a handwritten thank-you note from someone.

This is a dying art that really has so much impact so I encourage you to master this skill – if only because the rewards are so amazing. The habit of sending out thank you notes to people is not only a great way to show personal gratitude, it will also help you gain respect, trust, and stand out from the crowd. It is a simple way of showing gratitude toward someone who has done something kind for you.

You can send a thank you letter to anyone that deserves your thanks: whether it's a parent, friend, family member, trusted mentor or old boss, anyone who has helped you along the way. Writing a thank you note gives you a chance to think of the positive impact that person has had on your life and to share these feelings with him or her.

Here are some tips for writing a thank you letter:

- First and foremost, make sure you know how to spell their name properly in the greeting.

- Express your thanks. If you received a gift, make sure to mention it. Explain how much you appreciate the gift or opportunity.

- Be sincere and show enthusiasm.

- End your note with one more thank you.

- Always hand-write your note and use quality paper.

- If you would like to see a few sample thank you letters, search for examples online. There are hundreds! But don't copy them word or word. The most important thing about a thank you letter is that it speaks from the heart – YOUR HEART, that is.

85. HOW TO TALK TO PEOPLE

In today's world knowing how to talk to people is one of the most important skills you can possess. Don't think that's true? Then consider the alternative – if you aren't capable of communicating well then it's harder to make new friends, build a social life, form a relationship or move forward in your career.

Here are some simple tips on how to talk to people:

1. Ask Questions

This is the best conservational tool you can use to get other people to share information with you and engage in a conversation. Open-ended questions are great for keeping the conversation flowing. Avoid conversation-killers like politics and religion.

2. Listen

Remember the words SILENT and LISTEN are spelled with the same letters. When people speak do you actually listen or just wait patiently for a gap in the conversation for your turn to talk?

The biggest communication problem is that we don't listen to understand – we listen to reply. To truly listen you need to be SILENT. Listening means taking the time to consider what the other person is actually SAYING except you can't do this if you are talking or distracted at the same time. What is the person trying to tell you? What does he or she want you to understand?

It isn't about just hearing their words. You need to keep quiet and open your ears to the message other people are trying to give you. When you listen you have the opportunity to learn something new. So be patient and respectful, don't judge and take the time to THINK while you are silent. Other people appreciate being heard just as much as you do.

3. Share Information About Your Own Life

It is perfectly fine to open up and share relevant, appropriate information about yourself to others. You can keep it simple and avoid over-sharing so that the other person doesn't feel uncomfortable.

4. Know When To Keep Quiet

Sometimes there is a right time to keep quiet – you don't have to fill in every empty pause with chit-chat. If someone is giving you clear signs that they do not wish to carry on the conversation, it is probably best to end it.

5. Be Yourself

Don't try to be someone else. Talk about the things you love and are genuinely interested in. Smile and make eye contact. Tell a joke if you have just heard something funny. Nod your head if you agree with something. If you follow these tips and are sincere in your interactions, you may find that some strangers have the potential to become a friend.

86. HOW TO HAVE A CONVERSATION WITH SOMEONE OF ANY AGE

While it is great to have the ability to conserve with others, it is a sign of true maturity and humanity when a person can hold a quality conversation equally well with a 6 year old or an 80 year old person.

In life we tend to associate with people of a similar age, social standing, and cultural background. But when you open yourself up to embracing every age group and every human in this world, you grow in ways you never knew were possible.

Here are some important reasons why this skill should be mastered:

- With age comes wisdom. People who have already lived a long life often have so much great stuff to share with others. Ask them questions. Quiz them for advice. Delve into their minds!

- Embrace the young. Children see magic everywhere because they look for it. They laugh freely, are intensely curious and know how to play. Learn from them.

- Challenge your preconceptions. Don't assume that you know everything about a person. Everyone has something special to offer this world, whether they are young or old, from a different culture or country. Find out what it is.

- Show you care. Remember that everyone you meet in life is afraid of something, loves something and has lost something. Be open to hearing their story.

87. HOW TO TAKE RESPONSIBILITY

You need to understand that in life there won't always be someone there to save you. Your life is 100% your responsibility. As adults we still struggle with this, and believe me, there are some people who never grow up and insist on playing the blame game. Please do not be one of those people who think every little problem is the end of the world because it's not.

Some tips to help you master this skill:

- Responsibility is accepting that you are the cause and the solution of the matter.

- You need to be dependable and hold yourself accountable for your actions.

- Do the right thing. Apologise when you have made a mistake.

- Do what you set out to do with integrity.

- Accept responsibility for your actions. Be accountable for your results and take ownership of your mistakes.

- You are responsible for your own happiness. If you expect others to make you happy, chances are you will always end up disappointed.

- Everything in your life is a reflection of a choice you have made. If you want a different result, you need to make a different choice.

- You are free to do whatever you want, but you should always take responsibility for the consequences of the choices in your life.

- You cannot always change your circumstances but you can change yourself.

- The more you take responsibility for your past and present, the more you are able to create the future you seek.

88. HOW TO USE YOUR VOICE

Here's the thing – you have a voice so you should learn to use it, allow it to be heard, but in the right way. As John Grisham so wisely said:

In life, finding a voice is speaking and living the truth. Each of you is an original. Each of you has a distinctive voice. When you find it, your story will be told. You will be heard.

Words truly have the power to heal or harm, inspire or discourage others. You should be encouraged to speak up and communicate your thoughts and feelings, but in a tactful and considerate way. You should be encouraged to speak your truth and feel bold enough to share your voice with the world.

To use your voice, you need to first give yourself permission to speak up. Be proud of what you have to share. Even if you feel nervous and scared inside, you should always speak the truth. Your truth may not necessarily be someone else's – after all we are all entitled to our own opinions and thoughts. But you need to tell your own story because no one else can speak it for you.

So listen to your own voice, your own soul. Use your voice for kindness, your ears for compassion, your mind for truth, your hands for charity and your heart for love. Be true to the person you were created to be - do it for yourself.

You have something to say in this world. Something so true, so real, so you that it will ring unmistakably in the hearts of all who hear it. Are you willing to find your voice and say it?

Jacob Nordby.

89. HAVE GOOD SOCIAL SKILLS

Just as it is important to have good conversational skills, it is vital that you have good social skills too. This is important not only in the work environment, but in your personal life too.

Some important social skills to master:

- **ACCEPT PEOPLE ARE DIFFERENT**

  We are all individuals with different needs, strengths and weaknesses.

- **KNOW HOW TO BE A GOOD FRIEND TO OTHERS**

  To do this we need to be considerate and compassionate.

- **KNOW HOW TO COMMUNICATE AND WORK WITH OTHERS**

  To do this we need to be able to listen to, understand, respect, follow authorities and use our power wisely.

- **KNOW HOW TO BE A RESPECTFUL MEMBER OF THE COMMUNITY**

  To do this you must obey the laws and help others in the community, especially if all they need is a helping hand.

- **KNOW TO NURTURE YOUR FAMILY**

  To do this you will need to love and respect other family members and honor their differences.

- **ENCOURAGE AND COMPLIMENT OTHERS**

  Treat people as equals and encourage them to chase their dreams.

Here are some other social skills you will need to master.

HOW TO:

- Follow the steps
- Follow the rules
- Take turns
- Share materials
- How to wait patiently

- Listen to others

- Ignore distractions

- Stay calm with others

- Ask for help

- Be responsible for your own behavior

- Use proper body language

- Know the difference between being assertive and aggressive

- Disagree politely

- Accept criticism without being defensive.

- Show respect for others

90. HAVE MANNERS

The following is an excerpt from my book THE SMART KIDS GUIDE TO EVERYTHING, a book which details all the essential facts every child should know. Obviously manners are indispensable in civilized society and important if you wish to leave a favourable impression with others.

It's sad to see that people nowadays seem to have lost the fine art of etiquette. Manners are more than just knowing how to say please and thank you; it's the way in which you behave towards others. It's about considering the feelings of other people which is signified by the golden rule:

"Always do to others as you would wish them to do to you if you were in their place."

You can do this by trying to be the kind of person that is respectful and warm to others. It is also about following proper etiquette which is the proper and polite way to behave.

Here are some of the basic rules of good manners and correct etiquette:

- Knock on closed doors and wait to see if there is a response before entering.

- When you make a phone call introduce yourself first and then ask if you can speak with the person you are calling. For example: you can say "Is this a good time to speak?"

- Be appreciative and say "Thank You" for any gift you receive. You can even show your appreciation by writing a hand-written thank you note.

- Never use rude language in front of others. It only makes you look bad.

- Don't call people mean names or make fun of anyone for any reason. Teasing shows others you are weak and ganging up on someone else is cruel.

- Sit properly. Even if a play or assembly is boring sit through quietly and pretend that you are interested. The performers and presenters are doing their best.

- If you bump into somebody immediately say "excuse me".

- Cover your mouth when you cough or sneeze.

- Don't pick your nose in public.

- Hold the door open for people. As you walk through a door look around to see if you can hold it open for someone else.

- If you come across a parent, teacher or neighbour working on something ask if you can help. If they say yes then help. You might learn something new.

- When an adult asks you for a favour, do it without grumbling and with a smile.

- Say hello and goodbye.

- Say please and thank you.

- When someone helps you say thank you.

- Be on time.

- Know how to make a call.

- Clean up after you make a mess.

- Look people in the eye when you speak.

- Use respect when talking to adults.

- Don't interrupt.

- Say "excuse me" to get someone's attention.

- Wait your turn.

- Give compliments.

- Use kind words.

Manners at mealtimes

- Wash your hands before and after every meal.

- Place a napkin on your lap.

- Sit up straight and keep your elbows off the table.

- Chew with your mouth closed.

- Don't talk with your mouth full.

- Don't slurp or smack your lips while eating.

- Wipe your mouth with your napkin (not your sleeve!)

- Lean over your plate.

- Use the right utensils (don't eat with your hand).

- Offer to set the table.

- Learn to set the table appropriately.

- Don't complain about the food.

- Take your dishes to the sink when you have finished eating.

- Say please and thank you at the dinner table.

- Never say bad things about the food.

- Never stuff your mouth full of food.

- DO whatever you can to help prepare.

- Say "excuse me" if you burp.

- Don't talk loudly or interrupt when someone else is talking.

- Wait until everyone is served before starting to eat.

- If you have to sneeze, cough, blow your nose, or get something out of your teeth, go to the bathroom to do it.

- Don't point out other people's poor manners.

- If you have to leave the table during the meal say "excuse me".

- Do not take more than you can eat.

- Pass the food from left to right.

- Don't pick food up with your hands if you can use a fork.

- Eat small bites and swallow before taking another.

- Serve others before you serve yourself.

- Use your eating utensils properly. If you aren't sure then ask your parents to teach you or watch what other adults do.

- Keep a napkin on your lap. Use it to wipe your mouth when necessary.

- Don't reach for things at a table. Ask to have them passed.

Other important tips to remember

- Don't comment on someone's physical appearance unless you are giving a compliment.

- When someone asks you how you are doing, tell them then ask how they are doing.

- Write thank you notes for gifts you receive.

- Never use bad words.

- When you bump into someone say you are sorry.

- Offer help to those in need.

- Pick up after yourself, especially at someone else's house.

- Use your inside voice when you are indoors.

- Don't scream outside when you are playing, unless it's an emergency.

- Don't argue with adults.

- When someone is talking to you, look at them.

- Wait your turn to talk.

- Put down your electronics when someone enters the room.

- Shake hands firmly.

- Let others finish before you speak.

- Say "yes, ma'am" and "yes sir" when talking to grownups.

- Greet people with a "hi" or "how are you?"

- Ask before using.

- Ask before moving.

- Don't interrupt or yell out.

- Don't swear.

- Don't embarrass others.

If you are invited to a party

- Dress appropriately for the occasion.

- RSVP promptly. Always respond to an invitation after you receive it or acknowledge that you have got it. If you suddenly can't make it that's okay. Just make sure you give your host lots of notice.

- Never show up early or more than 15 minutes late.

- Don't bring along anyone else with you if they weren't invited. Or if you need to bring an extra person make sure you check first with the host to make sure that's okay. Don't just turn up with extra friends!

- Turn off your phone or electronics when speaking to other people.

GOOD MANNERS

To show respect and politeness please use these expressions when making requests:

WILL YOU?

Will you pass me the book?

WOULD YOU?

Would you pass me the book?

WOULD YOU PLEASE?

Would you please pass me the book?

COULD YOU PLEASE?

Could you please pass me the book?

COULD YOU POSSIBLY?

Could you possibly pass me the book?

WOULD YOU KINDLY?

Would you kindly pass me the book?

WOULD YOU MIND?

Would you mind passing me the book?

OR WOULD YOU BE SO KIND AS TO?

Would you be so kind as to pass me the book?

Also think about the WAY you speak. Remember to speak in a nice, kind tone instead of a mean or rude way.

91. HAVE AND TAKE THE INITIATIVE (TO DO STUFF!)

We have already looked at responsibility as a must-have skill but having and taking the initiative to do stuff is completely different. It means taking action *before* it is necessary. It means having the discipline to do the work *before* it needs to be done. It means looking for ways you can contribute to your own life and others and *actually doing something about it.*

So why is this skill so important to master? Because those who take some initiative in the workplace are high in demand. Employers want their staff to be proactive go-getters who know how to figure things out on their own. They want someone who doesn't need to be mollycoddled every step of the way. Life always finds a way to reward those who have and take the initiative to do stuff.

Some thoughts to keep in mind:

- If you want something in life, you are going to have to fight for it or chase it. Don't just assume it will fall into your lap.

- If your ship doesn't come in, maybe you should swim out to it.

- Challenge yourself to try new things every day. Who cares if you don't do things perfectly? Just be open to giving things a go.

- Make a conscious effort to give your absolute best to every task at hand. If you are going to give time to an activity, don't be half-assed about it. Do your best! At least try to do it well!

- Be persistent – if you fall down, get back up again. If you fall down again, pick yourself up one more time, brush off your knees and try again. The only way you are going to achieve your dreams is if you don't give up.

- Never give up on something you really want. It may be difficult to wait and keep trying but do you know what's even more difficult? Living with regret.

- Good things come to those who believe they deserve it. Better things come to those who are patient and the best things come to those who don't give up.

- The harder the struggle, the more glorious the triumph. Don't give up just because things are hard. Chasing your dreams will always have its hurdles, setbacks and struggles. Nothing worth having ever comes easy. Great things take both time and initiative.

92. UNDERSTAND THE VALUE OF A MISTAKE

Learning from failure teaches people tenacity, strength, patience, gumption, character, and makes one more capable of navigating life's inevitable ups and downs.

On the way to success you are going to make mistakes and IT'S OKAY! Failure is to be expected and embraced because that is how we learn – from making errors and learning what does and doesn't work. We all make mistakes – it's nothing to be embarrassed, anxious or nervous about. So don't be angry or upset when you make a mistake. It's just another lesson and opportunity for you to learn something new.

Here are some tips to learning the value of a mistake:

- It is not how we make mistakes but how we correct them that defines us.

- Don't waste time grieving over past mistakes. Learn from them and move on.

- Understand mistakes are a part of life. If you don't make them you will never learn or never improve.

- Your past mistakes are meant to guide you, not define you.

- Making mistakes is better than faking perfections.

- Every time you make a mistake you learn something new.

- Relationships grow stronger when both are willing to understand mistakes and forgive each other.

- Mistakes make us human. Failure makes us stronger. Hope keeps us going. Love keeps us alive.

93. HOW TO LET GO OF PAST GRIEVANCES

Let's face it – we all dwell on the past sometimes because we are human beings with emotion. But when our desire to cling on past grievances begins to impact our daily life and future, it is not only potentially unhealthy but a major roadblock that you need to work out how to get over.

Some important tips on how to let go of past grievances:

- It's okay to express your feelings. You are human. You are going to feel hurt, angry, disappointed and upset sometimes. But learn to do so in a non-accusing, constructive manner. Stop being a victim and blaming others – focus instead on how you can learn to forgive them and yourself.

- Focus more on the present instead of the past. Make the decision to let the past grievance go. What's done is done and can't be changed but you do have the power to positively impact your future.

- Understand that not everyone in your life is meant to stay forever. Some people come into your life just to teach you how to let go.

Your journey will be much lighter and easier if you don't carry and dwell on your past with you everywhere you go.

- Let it be what it is. When a thought is bringing you more misery than happiness, it is time to let go of that thought. When a person brings you more pain than joy, let them go. Don't miss your chance today of creating beautiful memories for tomorrow.

- Remember the quote by Esther Lederer: "Hanging onto resentment is letting someone you despise live rent-free in your head." Don't give them that privilege! Don't waste even one moment thinking about anyone who doesn't treat you with dignity and respect. They are definitely toxic and not worth your precious thoughts or headspace. Let life deal with the negative people – every bad action will eventually have its natural consequence.

- Become what you wish to be, without the burden of toxic people. Get rid of what you don't need. Allow change to shift. Stop holding onto holding that are meant to be gone. Let go of it instead.

- Have the courage to embrace the present. You can't start the next chapter of your life is you keep re-reading the last one. When you let go, something better is bound to come along. Go confidently in the direction of your dreams and live the life you always imagined.

94. HOW TO STAY CALM

There will be many moments in your life when you feel stressed and anxious, angry or upset. And all that tension has the potential to start a chain reaction of health problems which is why it is so important to learn how to stay calm when you are in the eye of a storm.

To become a master of calmness during a crisis:

- Take a deep breath. Get present in the moment and ask yourself what is really most important this very second.

- Pause and make sure you are thinking clearly enough so that you react appropriately.

- Assess the situation and decide what you should do next.

- Just because you are in a stressful situation doesn't mean you need to be stressed. Even if you are in a storm, it doesn't mean you need to let the storm get inside you.

- No matter how badly someone treats you, it doesn't mean you need to stoop to their level. Remain calm and strong and simply walk away.

- Focus on each day and moment at a time. Everything is manageable if you take it each step at a time.

- Stop worrying about what can go wrong. Instead get excited about what can go right. Worrying won't ever stop the bad stuff from happening. It just stops you from enjoying the good.

- Learn to control your thoughts so you don't create even more problems than what was there in the first place. Deal with the one problem at hand instead.

- Even then, accept that everything will eventually be okay. Calmness is not when you are in a place with no noise, trouble or hard work. It means to be in the midst of those things and inside you still have calm inside your heart.

- Remember the wise words of Dako: "just slow down. Slow down your speech. Slow down your breathing. Slow down your walking. Slow down your eating. And let this slower, steadier pace perfume your mind. Just slow down."

95. HOW TO NOT BE JUDGMENTAL

We are all inherently judgemental. It is human nature. We see someone and based on their looks or actions, we come to some sort of conclusion and this creates a division between us. Thankfully we can do our best to avoid passing judgement and instead work on building a bridge between two human beings.

To help you become less judgemental consider the following tips:

- Accept that everyone is different. We all have our own skeletons in our closet. Focus on your own life before being so quick to judge others.

- Understand that people are quick to judge others faults but are never quick to point out their own. Yet as the saying goes: "let he who is without sin, cast the first stone."

- Judging a person doesn't define who they are – it defines who you are. Everyone has the right to be who they are as an individual – they don't need to change for you.

- If you haven't walked in a person's shoes, then don't assume you know everything about that person.

- Instead of judging someone, try to understand the person. Try to imagine their background and the circumstances that might have led to the person acting or looking a particular way.

- Be more accepting of others, without trying to change them. People are who they are and you can't always change people. Accept people and situations for what they are, not what you want them to be.

- Show some love and compassion. Understand that being judgemental is not a behaviour that ultimately serves anyone.

BONUS SKILLS

96. HOW TO GROW YOUR OWN FOOD

Just because you don't have a big plot of land doesn't mean you can't grow your own food. Humans have been doing it for all of history – growing fruit, seeds and vegetables. Being able to master this skill usually equals increased health and confidence.

No matter whom you are or where you live, you can grow something to eat. Most of us have this idea in our heads it is hard work but you would be surprised to discover how much easier it is than we imagine it to be. There are whole books devoted to this topic but here are some simple ideas on how to master this skill:

- Start small and work out what space you have for this purpose. It is best to try to grow crops that don't require too much space, are productive, nutrient-dense and not too difficult to grow.

- Work out exactly which plants are the easiest to grow. This list includes: green bean, mint and other herbs, cherry tomatoes, cucumbers, lettuce and other salad greens, strawberries and mulberries.

- Plant a tree that yields fruit. These trees not only provide shade in the summers, they are actually perfect for producing many delicious fruits such as oranges, lemons, mandarins, figs and pomegranates.

- Even though eggs are technically not grown but laid, they are one of the world's healthiest foods and packed with protein, vitamins and minerals. Consider keeping some chickens in your backyard in order to boost self-sufficiency.

Those who have tasted organic, home-grown food understand full well that the intense flavour cannot be rivalled by anything found in the supermarket. There's a sense of pride that comes from planting a seed, watching it sprout and knowing that you have helped produce food for your family. This skill is rewarding in so many different ways.

97. HOW TO HAVE BASIC SURVIVAL SKILLS

We have probably all watched Survivor and wondered just how well we would fare if we were ever stranded on an island or forced to survive outside.

Skills that we are necessary for our survival in the wild:

1. **Locating a suitable place to stay**

   High and dry is best

2. **Where to find clean water**

   Grazing animals usually head to water near dawn and dusk and dew that hangs onto grass in a field is an excellent source of water)

3. **What you can and can't eat in the wild**

   For berries remember this simple mnemonic: *White and yellow - kill a fellow; purple and blue - good for you; red - could be good, could be dead.*

4. **How to navigate when lost**

5. **How to build a shelter**

6. **How to build a make-shift bed**

7. How to catch fish

8. How to keep your core temperature high

9. How to build a campfire

10. How to send up a survival signal

11. How to correctly cross a river or sea

If you haven't already mastered these core skills of wilderness safety, there's no time like the present to practice. Because you can read countless books and watch instructional videos but until you get out into the open, you won't actually know if all you have is a false sense of security. There is nothing like experience to give you a great boost of confidence.

98. HOW TO SPEAK IN FRONT OF OTHERS

On every Top Ten list of human fears, the fear of public speaking usually features in the number one spot. Amazingly it even beats the fear of dying, despite the fact we have been able to do since we were toddlers – that is, talk! For some reason the mere thought of doing it in front of a crowd, big or small, makes us feel sick, faint or sweaty.

Yet, sooner or later, it is a skill we have to master. Whether it's presenting a sales pitch or reciting a school speech, offering a toast or giving thanks at a special occasion, one day we are going to have bite the bullet and do it.

Some tips on how to feel comfortable speaking in front of others:

- Know that feeling scared is normal. As Mark Twain said, "there are two kinds of speakers – those that are nervous, and those that are liars."

- Understand it is a fear but like all fears it can be overcome with practice. Sure, you may feel totally nervous the first time (or first dozen times) you do it and maybe a little less anxious the next few but one day the fear will eventually subside or disappear.

- The best way to get better is to practice so check to see if you have a local Toastmasters club that you can attend. Don't be scared about going – that's where people go when they want to learn to conquer this fear! Or ask your family and friends to help you out by allowing you to practice speaking in front of them. Just stand up and speak about whatever topic comes to mind. Practicing impromptu speeches will make it easier to present prepared speeches later on.

- Of course having written notes or prompts are a massive help. Remember, you can think about what you want to say before you stand up to say it! Be sincere and brief. Speak from the heart. Once you have prepared words that you are comfortable with and properly convey your message, saying them out loud will feel so much easier.

- Worst case scenario you can practice in front of a mirror alone or even record yourself to see how you look or sound to others. You may feel stupid the first hundred times you do it but eventually the idea of speaking out loud will lose its crazy, scary hold on you.

Knowing how to speak in front of others is a huge asset that can help you both personally and professionally so do what you can to master it today.

99. KNOW YOUR RIGHTS

It is important that as citizens we know and practice our rights when appropriate, and enjoy the freedoms that our country has to offer. We all have rights but not all of us are aware of what they are exactly. This is important knowledge to have as we enter the world as fully culpable adults.

Some of our rights according to the Universal Declaration of Human Rights include:

1. We are all free and equal.

2. Right to no discrimination.

3. Right to life.

4. Right to no slavery.

5. Right to no torture.

6. We all have the same right to use the law.

7. We are all protected by the law.

8. Fair treatment by fair courts.

9. No unfair detainment.

10. The right to trial.

11. Innocent until proven guilty.

12. The right to privacy.

13. The right to a nationality.

14. The right to marry and have a family.

15. The right to own things or share them.

16. Freedom of thought.

17. Freedom to say what you want.

18. Freedom to meet where we like.

19. The right to democracy.

20. The right to social security.

21. Worker's right – we have the right to a fair wage.

22. .The right to play and have rest.

23. The right to an education.

24. Right to culture and copyright.

25. A free and fair world.

26. Nobody can take these rights and freedoms from us.

100. HOW TO PICK THE RIGHT PARTNER

As a teenager, one quote imprinted on my mind the moment my eyes scanned across the words. It was by H. Jackson Brown Jr who said: "Choose your life's mate carefully. From this one decision will come 90 per cent of all your happiness or misery."

Teenagers are well known for their amazing ability to fall deeply and swiftly in love. They often experience intense feelings of attraction for the opposite sex and these feelings can be ignited from something as simple as a cute smile or crinkly, sweet eyes. Sometimes these feelings are reciprocated, other times kids get totally crushed by their crush.

The problem is they don't teach this stuff at school and we don't always have the relationship know-how ourselves. Nonetheless there's no greater skill than this: knowing how to identify a good relationship, pick the right partner and keep the love and respect alive after the honeymoon period has passed.

This one decision – picking the right partner – has the power to influence our life even more than our career. Of course, it is important to precursor this discussion by noting no relationship or person is perfect in this world. In addition to this, you should know what to look for and avoid in a partner, and how to be a good partner in return.

Relationships improve with experience with guidance and you can learn to avoid some common pitfalls and mistakes that are bound to occur in dating and relationships.

Here are some other important points to consider (from my book INSPIRING TEENS: HOW TO LIVE A LIFE WITHOUT REGRET):

- Love isn't supposed to make you feel insecure, ashamed or embarrassed to be you. It isn't supposed to make you feel like you are "not enough".

- Real love is reciprocated and generous. It is sweet and kind.

- People who are in love with you don't play silly games. They don't cheat or lie to you.

- They don't intentionally treat you terribly either or set out to make you jealous.

- Most important of all, they don't physically or emotionally hurt you.

- Instead they are respectful of your feelings. They make you feel valued, cared for and special.

You need to know that if love is making you cry all the time it isn't right. No person is worth your tears and when you find the right one he or she won't make you cry. You don't have to go chasing love – be patient and it will find you.

SIMPLE BITE-SIZE ADVICE ON
HOW TO HAVE CONFIDENCE

- Know that confidence is when what YOU think of yourself is more important than what OTHER PEOPLE think of you.

- Stop comparing yourself to others. Stay focused on you. Life is too short to waste your time trying to be someone else.

- Love yourself because you are a gift. Nothing would be the same if you didn't exist.

- Be positive and look for the good in every situation.

- Instead of wishing you were someone else, be proud of who you are. You never know who is looking at you wishing they were you,

- Confidence is not "they will like me." Confidence is "I'll be fine if they don't.

- Confidence means believing in yourself even when no one else does.

- Confidence may not bring success but it gives power to face any challenge.

- The best way to gain self-confidence is to do what you are afraid to do.

- There's no need to be perfect to inspire others. Let others get inspired by how you deal with your imperfections.

- Confidence is like a muscle – the more you use it, the stronger it gets.

- Talk to yourself like you would to someone you love.

- Confidence is something you create within yourself by believing in who you are.

- Jealously is just a lack of self-confidence.

- If you are confident, you are beautiful.

- Be yourself because everyone else is taken.

- Be who you are, not who the world wants you to be.

- When you doubt your power, you give power to your doubt.

- True confidence has no room for jealously and envy. When you know you are great, you have no reason to hate.

- Lack of confidence can put you in an emotionally bad place so believe in yourself.

- Self-confidence is the foundation of all great success and achievement.

- One of the greatest challenges in life is being yourself in a world that's trying to make you like everyone else.

- Second guessing yourself indicates a lack of confidence and a lack of confidence means you have no faith and no faith equals failure.

- If you don't have confidence you will always find some excuse not to try or win.

- Never change who you are because someone else has a problem with it.

- If you want to fly, give up everything that weighs you down.

- Stop beating yourself up. You are a work in progress which means you get there a little at a time, not all at once.

- A clear vision backed by definite plans gives you a tremendous feeling of confidence and personal power.

- Remember you are braver than you believe, stronger than you seem and smarter than you think.

APPENDIX: LIFE SKILLS
REFERENCE GUIDE

Under 5 Life Skills

- Put dirty clothes into a laundry hamper

- Help sort dirty clothes into color piles

- Help feed the pet

- Get the mail

- Pick up toys

- Empty dishwasher and put dishes away

Age 6-10 Life Skills

ALL OF THE ABOVE, PLUS:

- Organize own drawers and closet

- Empty dishwasher and put dishes away

- Wash and dry dishes by hand

- Straighten up living and family rooms

- Rake leaves

- Help put groceries away

- Make a sandwich and toast

- Pour milk or juice into a cup or onto cereal

- Wash out plastic trash cans

- Clean mirrors and windows

- Run own shower or bath

- Clean windows

- Empty kitchen trash

- Use a vacuum cleaner

- Clean pet cages and food bowls

- Use a broom and dustpan

- Sweep porches and decks

- Answer the telephone

- Take a written phone message

- Learn basic food groups and good nutrition habits

- Read and prepare a simple recipe

- Make hard and soft boiled eggs

- Pack lunchboxes into schoolbag

- Cut up own food

- Water plants

- Strip sheets off bed

- Straighten up book and toy shelves

- Fold clothes neatly

- Water house plants and lawn outside

- Wipe bathroom sink

- Load and turn on dishwasher

- Trim own nails and clean own ears

- Set table correctly

- Mop floor

- Peel vegetables

- Understand basic time management skills

- Load and operate washing machine and dryer

- Fold blankets neatly

- Straighten and organize kitchen drawers and refrigerator

- Prepare hot beverages

- Dust household furniture

- Count money and give change

Age 10-12 Life Skills

ALL OF THE ABOVE, PLUS:

- Peg washing on the line

- Take washing off the line

- Fold washing and put it away

- Remake own bed with clean sheets

- Bake a cake or pancakes from scratch

- Help with cooking dinner

- Make a green salad and dressing

- Cook hot dogs and scrambled eggs

- Grill meat

- Understand the importance of ingredient and nutrient labelling

- Know how to select and prepare fruits and vegetables

- Know basic emergency first-aid procedures

- Understand uses of medicine and seriousness of overuse

- Understand basic money management

- Clean oven and stove

- Pull weeds from the garden

- Do simple mending and sew on buttons

- Understand basics of camera use

- Take pet for a walk

Ages 13 to 15 Life Skills

ALL OF THE ABOVE, PLUS:

- Replace light bulbs

- Iron clothes

- Wash and polish a car

- Maintain a bicycle – fill tires with air and oil squeaks

- Make grocery lists

- Shop for groceries

- Make dinners alone

- Make deposits and withdrawals at the bank

- Perform basic first aid and CPR

- Manage a day of activities

- Learn to touch-type

Ages 16 to 18 Life Skills

ALL OF THE ABOVE, PLUS:

- Plan well-balanced meals, including shopping and cooking

- Pass a driver's test

- Volunteer

- Have a work experience (paid or unpaid) with responsibilities and set hours.

- Do simple home repairs

- Fill out a job application

- Watch younger siblings

- Make one complete meal

- Prepare a resume

NOTE FOR PARENTS OF
CHILDREN WITH SPECIAL NEEDS

Before this book comes to an end, I think it's important to include a note for parents of children with special needs. As a mother of two children, one of whom has a degenerative neuro-muscular condition, I understand full well that not every child or young adult will be able to master all the skills included this book.

Under these circumstances, I think it is important that children start where they are, use what they have and do what they can. In my book THEY SAY I'M SPECIAL: 100 TIPS FOR RAISING A HAPPY AND RESILIENT CHILD WITH SPECIAL NEEDS I identified numerous ways in which a parent could help boost their child's confidence, especially when they are not able to do so in the traditional way.

You will need to identify your child's strengths and work out what they are capable of doing. Can they help oversee and manage any activities? Can they assist in making decisions on meal-planning or purchases? Can they offer their opinions, ideas or thoughts on a subject matter? Can they become experts on a topic that interests them?

Every child has his or her own strengths and has something special to offer so you will need to tailor their personal tasks and skill-building exercises to their individual abilities. Do not do for your children what they can do for themselves.

Remember every child wants to feel competent and smart. Even children with special needs have a desire to feel needed and valuable, just like everyone else. Just as able-bodied kids grow confident when they gain new skills, children with special needs also benefit from the opportunity to assert their independence.

So look for different ways that you can make this happen as self-confidence is the foundation of all great success and achievement. As a wise person once said, "The simple goal of being a family, of parenting our children, doesn't really look any more complicated than this: Raise them well equipped to leave home and to establish faithful lives that are both fulfilling and self-sufficient."

PARENTING WISDOM COLLECTION

- Don't worry that children never listen to you; worry that they are always watching you. *Robert Fulghum*

- Every child is gifted. They just unwrap their packages at different times. *Unknown*

- If you have never been hated by your child you have never been a parent. *Bette Davis*

- Each day of our lives we make deposits in the memory banks of our children. *Charles R. Swindall*

- There is no such thing as a perfect parent. So just be a real one. *Sue Atkins*

- The way we talk to our children becomes their inner voice. *Peggy O'Mara*

- Children are great imitators. So give them something great to imitate.

- Children need love, especially when they do not deserve it. *Harold Hulbert*

- Tell me and I forget. Teach me and I remember. Involve me and I learn. *Benjamin Franklin*

- Don't let yourself become so concerned with raising a good kid that you forget you already have one. *Glennon Melton*

- One of the most important things we adults can do for children is to MODEL the kind of person we would like them to be. *Carol B. Hillman*

- 5 questions to ask yourself when parenting young adults: Are my parenting strategies:

    o Moving toward independence?
    o Balancing freedom and responsibility?
    o Motivated primarily by love or fear?
    o Providing guidance without enabling?
    o Part of an ongoing dialogue? *Julie Hanks*

- Parenting is the easiest thing in the world to have an opinion about, but the hardest thing in the world to do. *Matt Walsh*

- I believe that children are our future. Teach them well and let them lead the way. Show them all the beauty they possess inside. Give them a sense of pride. *Whitney Houston*

- Enjoy the little things, for one day you may look back and realise they were the big things. *Robert Brault*

- One generation full of deeply loving parents would change the brain of the next generation, and with that, the world. Dr. *Charles Raison*

- Treat a child as though he already is the person he's capable of becoming. *Haim Ginott*

- Encourage and support your kids because children are apt to live up to what you believe of them. *Lady Bird Johnson*

- Life affords no greater responsibility, no greater privilege, than the raising of the next generation. *C. Everett Koop*

- Let's raise children who won't have to recover from their childhoods. *Pam Leo*

- Behind the child that makes the most progress is an actively involved parent.

- Your kids watch you for a living. It's their job; it's what they do. That's why it's so important to try your best to be a good role model. *James Lehman*

- We worry about what a child will become tomorrow, yet we forget that he is someone today. *Stacia Taucher*

- Do the best you can until you know better. Then when you know better, do better. *Maya Angelou*

- It's not what you do for your children, but what you have taught them to do for themselves, that will make them successful human beings. *Ann Landers*

OTHER BOOKS BY FRANCES VIDAKOVIC

Non-Fiction

- Lightbulb Moments: 50 Aha! Insights That Will Transform Your Life

- Inspiring Teens: How To Live A Life Without Regret

- Happy Thoughts: 200 Inspiring Quotes Explained for Kids and Teens

- Life is An Experiment: I Dare You To Live It

- The Smart Kids Guide to Everything

- Create a Life You Love

- They Say I'm Special: 100Tips for Raising a Happy and Resilient Child with Special Needs

- When He's A Keeper: But You Feel Like Throwing Him Away

- Croatian Princess: A Collection of Musings

Fiction

- Before I Die: A Pact

- Just A Little Break

- Pretty Mansnatchers

- Enchanted Island

- When I Fall Again

.

Manufactured by Amazon.ca
Bolton, ON

13777144R00146